Statutory Audits in Europe

In the aftermath of the Global Financial Crisis, corporate collapses, accounting scandals, and concerns around competition and auditor choice, the European Commission (EC) promoted the preparation of various reports on audit policy to support a harmonisation process of European auditing regulation. Consequently, the European Union (EU) Audit Regulation and Directive was implemented from 2016.

This book provides a timely picture of the audit sector and how it responds to regulatory and technological challenges. It analyses the impact of EU reforms on audit practices by comparing the UK and Italy, which, representing two very different regulatory and cultural contexts, will offer insight into how the efforts at standardising audit regulation may lead to very different organisational firm responses within Europe. It addresses issues relating to public policy work and the concerns faced by the market for audit and assurance services, in promoting audit quality, better communication about the role of the auditor, capital market stability and confidence, and auditor independence. Moreover, it highlights what the future of auditing might look like in the EU particularly now that the UK has left, and how meeting public expectations will continue to be a struggle for the accounting profession given the many problems ahead.

The book encourages a deeper awareness of the challenges faced by those that monitor and certify the financial statements of the world's largest public companies and contributes to the general understanding of this controversial industry. It will serve as a useful guide to the recent EU audit reforms, not only for academics, and research students but also to regulators, policymakers, standard setters, industry professionals, and business executives worldwide.

Michael Kend, PhD, is a lecturer of accounting in the School of Accounting, Information Systems and Supply Chain at RMIT University, Australia.

Giulia Leoni, PhD, is associate professor of accounting at the University of Genoa, Italy.

Cristina Florio, PhD, is associate professor of accounting at the University of Verona, Italy.

Silvia Gaia, PhD, is a reader in accounting at Essex Business School (University of Essex, UK).

Routledge Studies in Accounting

Business Models and Corporate Reporting
Defining the Platform to Illustrate Value Creation
Lorenzo Simoni

Accounting and Auditing Standards for Islamic Financial Institutions
Mohd Ma'Sum Billah

Quality Management and Accounting in Service Industries
A New Model of Quality Cost Calculation
Wojciech Sadkowski and Piotr Jedynak

Artificial Intelligence in Accounting
Organisational and Ethical Implications
Othmar Lehner and Carina Knoll

The Financial Reporting Quality of Public Companies
The Cultural Dimension
Katarzyna Mokrzycka-Kogut

Strategic Pricing and Management Accounting
David Dugdale

Statutory Audits in Europe
Latest Reforms and Future Challenges
Michael Kend, Giulia Leoni, Cristina Florio and Silvia Gaia

For more information about this series, please visit www.routledge.com/Routledge-Studies-in-Accounting/book-series/SE0715

Statutory Audits in Europe

Latest Reforms and Future Challenges

Michael Kend, Giulia Leoni, Cristina Florio and Silvia Gaia

Routledge
Taylor & Francis Group
LONDON AND NEW YORK

First published 2023
by Routledge
4 Park Square, Milton Park, Abingdon, Oxon OX14 4RN

and by Routledge
605 Third Avenue, New York, NY 10158

Routledge is an imprint of the Taylor & Francis Group, an informa business

British Library Cataloguing-in-Publication Data
A catalogue record for this book is available from the British Library

Library of Congress Cataloging-in-Publication Data
Names: Kend, Michael, author. | Leoni, Giulia, author. | Florio, Cristina, author. | Gaia, Silvia, author.
Title: Statutory audits in Europe : latest reforms and future challenges / Michael Kend, Giulia Leoni, Cristina Florio and Silvia Gaia.
Description: Abingdon, Oxon ; New York, NY : Routledge, 2023. | Series: Routledge studies in accounting | Includes bibliographical references and index. | Contents: Introduction—Institutional setting and audit regulation in Europe—New audit reports : improving informational content and value—Mandatory auditor firm rotation (MAFR) : perceived benefits and costs—Restrictions and caps on non-audit work : challenges and response strategies—Audit committees : greater powers and proposed standards—The future of audit : impacts of new technologies—The new paths of statutory audits in Europe : meeting public expectations and other future challenges.
Identifiers: LCCN 2022045744 (print) | LCCN 2022045745 (ebook) | ISBN 9781032201733 (hardback) | ISBN 9781032201740 (paperback) | ISBN 9781003262596 (ebook)
Subjects: LCSH: Auditing—Law and legislation—European Union countries.
Classification: LCC KJE2491 .K46 2023 (print) | LCC KJE2491 (ebook) | DDC 346.4/06648—dc23/eng/20230105
LC record available at https://lccn.loc.gov/2022045744
LC ebook record available at https://lccn.loc.gov/2022045745

ISBN: 978-1-032-20173-3 (hbk)
ISBN: 978-1-032-20174-0 (pbk)
ISBN: 978-1-003-26259-6 (ebk)

DOI: 10.4324/9781003262596

Typeset in Sabon
by codeMantra

Contents

List of illustrations

Figures

Tables

Acknowledgements

The financial support of the Institute of Chartered Accountants in England and Wales (ICAEW's) charitable trusts is gratefully acknowledged. The authors would like to thank Professor Lee Parker from University of Glasgow for his invaluable observations which helped to improve the book, and thank Professor Alessandro Lai and Professor Silvano Corbella, both from the University of Verona, for their support and advice during our data collection phase.

Acknowledgements

About the authors

Michael Kend, PhD, is a lecturer in the School of Accounting, Information Systems and Supply Chain at RMIT University, Australia. He has studied and researched audit and assurance markets for more than 18 years. He spent several months working in the UK during the years 2016, 2017, and 2018 on research related to the impact of the Brexit decision on UK audits and on audit market concentration in the UK. He has research experience covering archival, empirical, and interview-based research. Previously he completed work on an ARC Linkage Grant funded by the Australian government and is best known for his research book titled *The Future of Audit: Keeping Capital Markets Efficient* published in 2010. He also completed a funded project for the ICAEW in 2021, which produced the report titled *EU Audit Reforms: Analysing Different Impacts in the UK and Italy*. He has published several studies in leading business journals, such as *ABACUS, International Journal of Auditing, Critical Perspectives on Accounting and Accounting and Finance*. He has been awarded several external grants including from the ICAEW, CPA Australia, CA ANZ, ARC Linkage, and the AFAANZ research grants scheme.

Giulia Leoni, PhD, is associate professor of accounting at the University of Genoa, Italy. Her research engages with accounting and accountability in diverse settings, especially in the digital realm; with risk management and audit reforms; and with accounting history. Her singled and co-authored works are published in *Accounting, Auditing, and Accountability Journal, British Accounting Review, Meditari Accounting Research, Accounting History, Journal of Management History* and *Critical Perspectives on Accounting*. She serves as editorial board member for *Accounting, Auditing, and Accountability Journal, Accounting History,* and has acted and acts as guest editor for special issues of the same journals. She is the chair of the Special Interest Group of Accounting History of the Accounting and Finance Association of Australia and New Zealand (AFAANZ).

Cristina Florio, PhD, is associate professor of accounting at the University of Verona, Italy. Her research interests include accounting, auditing, and enterprise risk management. She has research experience covering archival, empirical, and interview-based research. She has published her research in highly ranked journals like *Accounting Forum*, *British Accounting Review*, *Journal of International Accounting, Auditing and Taxation* (*JIAAT*), *Journal of International Accounting Research* and *Meditari Accountancy Research*. She has authored several books and book chapters and acted as book editor. She is an editorial board member of the *JIAAT*. Cristina completed a funded project for the ICAEW in 2021, which resulted in the publication of the report *EU Audit Reforms: Analysing Different Impacts in the UK and Italy*. She also participated in research projects funded by the Italian Ministry for Research (MIUR). She was a panellist in a workshop organised by the Italian Securities and Exchange Commission (CONSOB) on audit issues. Cristina serves the *American Accounting Association* (*AAA*) as International Council Member-At-Large (2021–2023) and the *AAA International Accounting Section* as member of the Advisory Board.

Silvia Gaia, PhD, is a reader in accounting at Essex Business School (University of Essex, UK). Silvia's research work mainly relates to corporate governance, financial and non-financial accounting, and reporting. She has relevant experience in archival, empirical, and quantitative research and in comparative studies. She has published her research in highly reputed academic journals such as *Accounting, Auditing and Accountability Journal*, *Accounting Forum*, *British Accounting Review*, *European Journal of Finance*, *Journal of Business Ethics*, and *International Business Review*, among others. She is an editorial board member of *Accounting Forum* and *Journal of Accounting in Emerging Economies*. Silvia is currently the Chair of the Special Interested Group of the British Accounting and Finance Association (BAFA) on Financial Accounting and Reporting (FARSIG). She has been awarded several external grants from different bodies, including the Basildon Borough Council, British Academy, Financial Reporting Council, ICAEW, and Institute of Family Business.

Executive summary

Evidence has been limited on the impacts of the Directive (2014/56/EU) and Regulation (537/2014) – altogether, EU Audit Reform (2014) – on European auditors, especially with respect to the regulatory, economic, and cultural differences amongst European countries. This book provides insights on the direct consequences of the 2014 EU Audit Reform for auditors and other participants in the audit and assurance market using a comparative perspective. This book compares the differential impacts of these reforms on the organisational management and audit practices of audit practitioners in both the UK and Italy. The UK and Italy are purposively selected as representing two very different institutional settings, which will offer insights on how the efforts at standardising audit regulation may lead to very different organisational firm responses within Europe. Further, we have surveyed auditors throughout Europe to extend the findings and further bring context on the impacts of technology on audit practices and the future of audit. We used focus groups or office interviews in major business cities and regional centres such as London, Edinburgh, Milan, Rome, and Verona, to capture as wide a range of relevant opinions as possible from larger and smaller audit practitioners and other stakeholders such as regulators, standard setters, company management and directors, investors, and professional bodies. Speaking with auditors enabled the authors to understand the underlying arguments, approaches, opinions, and procedures related to the issues under investigation, and ultimately to link the results to a social context. We then surveyed around 85 European auditors in 2022 to gain further insights into some of the issues first raised during 2017, 2018, and 2019.

The ultimate and overarching conclusions of this book are that, after several successive EU interventions to regulate and harmonise audit practices in the audit and assurance markets throughout the EU, the process of harmonisation remains difficult to achieve because of the significant differences that characterise countries within the EU. Indeed, European countries such as the UK and Italy have significant institutional and cultural differences that affect how such implementation of EU Directives take place, and this book reports differences in how the latest EU Audit Reforms (2014) have impacted these two very different EU countries. Future research should consider collecting more field data on the specific reforms to audit such as the extended auditors' report, the audit tendering process, and the non-audit service caps/restrictions from other EU countries. By investigating how these EU reforms have impacted auditors at a macro level where changes to local audit markets are considered, more details could emerge that will help to further explain some of the present findings we report related to the UK and Italy.

1 Introduction

1.1 Introduction

Over the last decade or so, the European Union (EU) has favoured the harmonisation of audit requirements for public interest entities (PIEs) and introduced a wide set of rules covering the provision of audit and non-audit services (NAS), audit reports, and auditor tenure. Currently, very little is known on audit firms' implementation of this EU Audit Reform and how it affects auditor practice and overall performance (Maijoor and Vanstraelen, 2012). More knowledge is needed to assess the impacts of changes in audit practices imposed by regulatory intervention, and whether such intervention ultimately leads to a more consistent audit quality for these firms across countries (Maijoor and Vanstraelen, 2012). By considering the views of auditors and other key stakeholders, this book provides insights on the impact of EU Audit Reform on audit practices, and thus will assist policymakers and professional accounting bodies in assessing the impact of regulatory interventions on auditor behaviour and practice, whilst also better informing the investor public.

A comparison of different institutional settings is deemed to be useful for gaining a better understanding of issues such as the standardisation/harmonisation of auditing standards and of auditing practices in a globalised economy (Needles, 1989; Schilder, 1996). This is especially deemed useful for drawing relevant insights for policymakers and practitioners regarding their impacts. Previous international studies on auditing practices (e.g., Kend and Basioudis, 2018) have shown how past European reforms and recommendations, e.g., "Statutory Auditors' Independence in the EU: A Set of Fundamental Principles" (EC, 2000), have been implemented with a significant degree of difference in nations such as France, Italy, and the UK due to the relevant cultural differences among these countries (Stevenson, 2002). In this book, we aim at analysing the impact of EU reforms on audit practices and offer insights on how the efforts at standardising audit regulation may lead to very different organisational firm responses within Europe. For instance, some countries have implemented the minimum EU requirements, but others have kept or even newly included additional

DOI: 10.4324/9781003262596-1

entities to their national PIEs' definition. There is still a wide diversity of definitions of PIEs applicable across European countries, although the EU Audit Reform (2014) has helped in more harmonisation.

To achieve these aims, this book will first provide an overview of the evolution of audit practices in Europe before and after the enactment of the EU Audit Reform. It will then empirically analyse the overall impacts of these reforms in two very different European regulatory and cultural contexts, the UK and Italy, and consider the perceptions of large and small audit practitioners in doing so.

We focus on the UK and Italy for several reasons. They represent, respectively, the second and the fourth largest European economies in terms of gross domestic product (International Monetary Fund, 2018). In the UK there is a preference for applying judgement rather than strict rules, for questioning authority and being more supportive of social equality. The UK is a principle-based jurisdiction based on the "comply or explain" approach, whereby companies are encouraged to comply with regulations or explain why they are not complying. In Italy, accounting practices are regulated according to a rules-based system, where rules are released via decrees and included in the Italian Civil Code, where questioning of authority rarely occurs and is not encouraged. In recent times, with three subsequent regulations (Law 262/2005, Legislative Decree 303/2006, and Legislative Decree 39/2010), Italy modified its long-standing provisions on mandatory audit firm rotation, renewable mandate terms, and cooling-off periods. Italy also introduced audit partner rotation in conjunction to audit firm rotation. The UK and Italy have responded to corporate collapses, accounting scandals, and the Global Financial Crisis (GFC) by issuing new rules on corporate governance and audit, albeit by focusing on different mechanisms. The Carillion collapse (UK) in 2017 raised concerns related to external auditor oversight and Grant Thornton's decision to stop bidding for UK tenders involving large companies also raised questions regarding the effectiveness of the EU Audit Reform and audit market competition (Marriage, 2018). The UK accountancy firms and the Financial Reporting Council (FRC) have faced renewed scrutiny from the investor public and the UK government because of these matters.

In summary, this book aims at addressing issues related to public policy work and the challenges faced by the market for audit and assurance services, in promoting audit quality, better communication about the role of the auditor, capital market stability and confidence, and auditor independence. Moreover, it intends to provide insights on the future of the audit profession in Europe and its regulation. The insights from the book will generate better awareness of these challenges faced by those that monitor and certify the financial statements of the world's largest public companies. In the next section, we present a timeline of the EU Audit Reforms measures, effectively starting from the 2003 Action Plan related to Company Law and Governance and ending with the more recent implementation in June 2016 of the EU Audit Directive (2014/56/EU) and Regulation (537/2014).

1.2 The EU Audit Reforms (2003–2016)

Over the last decade or so, the EU has favoured harmonisation of audit requirements for PIEs and introduced a wide set of rules covering the provision of audit and NAS. In the aftermath of the GFC, corporate collapses, accounting scandals, and concerns around competition and auditor choice, the European Commission (EC) initiated an extensive consultation with the launch of the "Green Paper on Audit Policy: Lessons from the Crisis." Following four years of negotiations, an amended Directive (2014/56/EU) and a new Regulation (537/2014) were formally signed on 16 April 2014, becoming effective as of June 2016, known as the EU Audit Reform 2014 (Ratzinger-Sakel and Schönberger, 2015; Horton et al., 2018). Figure 1.1 is a timeline of the EU reform agenda since 2003.

2003 – On 21 May 2003, the EC adopted an Action Plan for modernising Company Law and Corporate Governance at EU level (Action Plan):

> The main objectives of the 2003 action plan were: (1) to strengthen shareholders' rights; and (2) to protect employees, creditors and other parties with which companies deal. The EC made it a priority as part of its 2003 Action Plan to encourage the coordination and convergence of national codes through regular high-level meetings of what was then called The European Corporate Governance Forum (DG 2003). The Action Plan is based on a comprehensive and prioritised set of proposals for action, covering several years. It devotes special attention to a series of corporate governance initiatives aimed at boosting confidence in capital markets (DG 2003). It was open to public consultation for three months.

2006 – Release of Directive 2006/43/EC of the European Parliament and of the Council of 17 May 2006 on statutory audits of annual accounts and consolidated accounts:

> The Directive 2006/43/EC of the European Parliament and of the Council of 17 May 2006 on statutory audits of annual accounts and consolidated accounts (also known as the 8th EU Company Law Directive on Statutory Audits) amended Council Directives 78/660/EEC and 83/349/EEC and repealed Council Directive 84/253/EEC. The major objective of this European Directive was to establish the rules concerning the statutory audit of annual and consolidated accounts. This revised EU Directive extends the scope of application of existing EU legislation in the audit field (EU Directive 84/253/EEC – repealed), by: (1) mentioning more clearly the duties of statutory auditors, and the criteria for independence and professional ethics; (2) introducing new requirements for providing external quality assurance by adopting a better public oversight over the audit professionals; and (3) stimulating the cooperation among various oversight bodies within the European context (EC 2010).

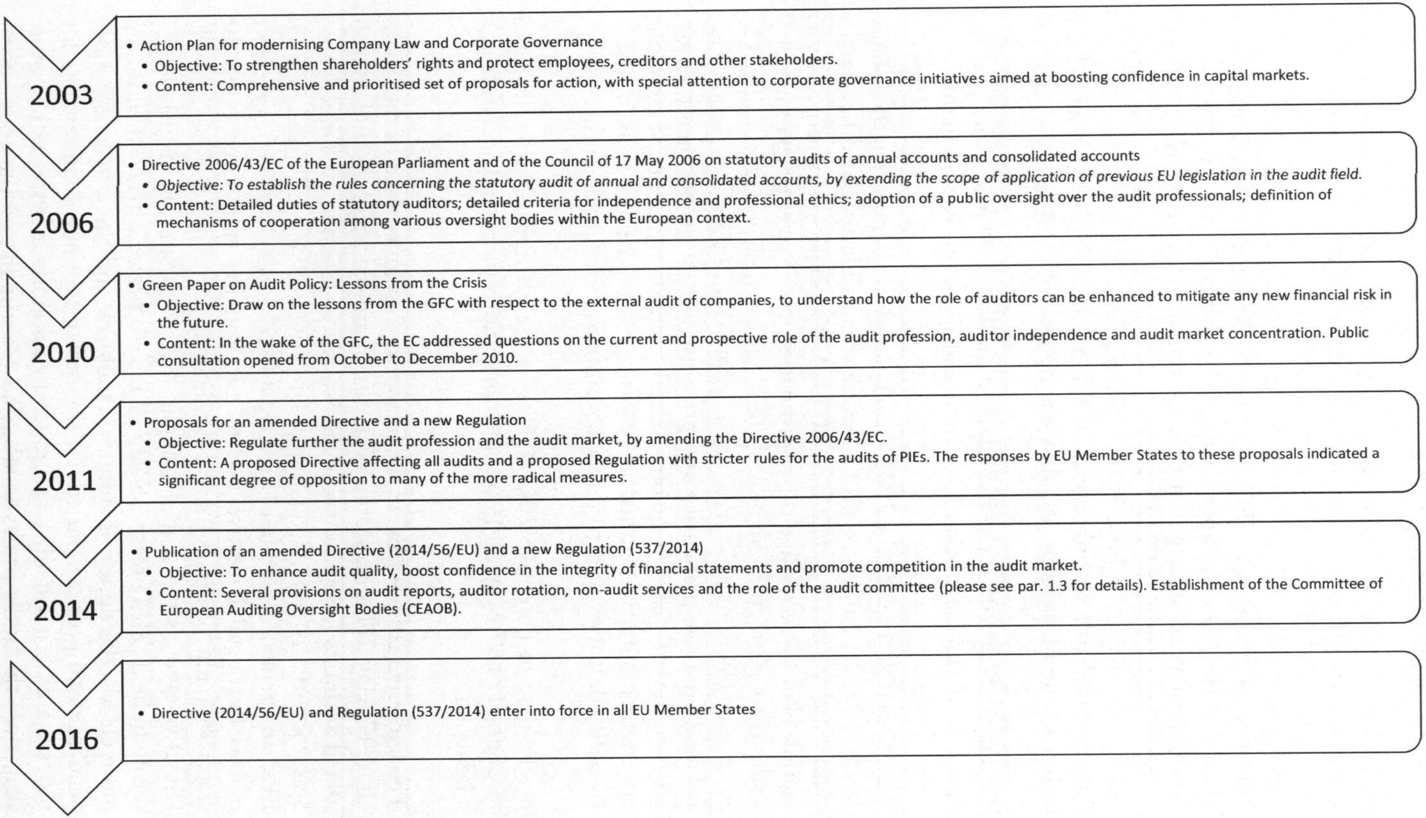

Figure 1.1 A timeline of the EU Audit Reforms (2003–2016).

2010 – The EC launches the "Green Paper on Audit Policy: Lessons from the Crisis":

> The Green Paper aimed to draw on the lessons from the GFC with respect to the external audit of companies. It was open to public consultation for three months (October 2010 to December 2010). In the wake of the financial crisis, the EC needed to ask the question of whether the role of auditors can be enhanced to mitigate any new financial risk in the future (EC 2010). The crisis also highlighted certain weaknesses in the audit sector which needed to be explored further. In the Green Paper, the EC was seeking, among other things, to address three broad questions: (1) what the current role of the audit profession is and whether it should change; (2) whether the profession is sufficiently independent from the companies that it audits; and (3) whether the audit market is excessively concentrated. The EC was keen to discuss whether audits provide the right information to all financial actors, whether there are issues around the independence of audit firms, whether there are risks linked to a concentrated market, whether supervision at a European level might be useful, and how best the specific needs of small- and medium-sized businesses may be met (EC 2010).

2011 – The EC adopts two proposals, i.e., an amended Directive and a new Regulation:

> The European Commission (EC) proposed two pieces of legislation that affect the audit profession and the audit market. The first was a proposed Directive that would concern all audits, while the provisions in the proposed Regulation would apply to the audits of PIEs (EC 2016). PIEs are listed companies and certain other public-interest organizations such as unlisted credit institutions. The more extreme provisions being proposed by the EC are contained in the Regulation. The proposals of 30 November 2011 would in some ways amend, and in other ways build, upon the 8th EU Company Law Directive on Statutory Audits (2006). EU Member States' responses to the EC's legislative proposals indicated a significant degree of opposition to many of the more radical measures (EC 2017). With that degree of opposition, it was unlikely that the EC's legislative proposals could be adopted in their current form.

2014 – An amended Directive (2014/56/EU) and a new Regulation (537/2014) are formally signed:

> The amended Directive and new Regulation both aim at enhancing audit quality and at promoting competition in the audit market. The reform of the EU audit legislation came into being to boost confidence

in the integrity of financial statements (EU 2014a, 2014b). Article 27 of Regulation (537/2014) serves as a means of effectively and regularly monitoring compliance with these aims. Among others, Article 27 deals with the monitoring of the following aspects of the EU market for the provision of statutory audit services to PIEs: (1) market concentration levels; (2) risks to audit quality and measures to mitigate these; and (3) the performance of audit committees. Moreover, Article 30 of Regulation (537/2014) provided for the establishment of the Committee of European Auditing Oversight Bodies (CEAOB) as a new framework for co-operation between national audit oversight bodies at the EU level. From the period 2011–2014, the EU Commission also investigated several audit issues and developed the EU Audit Directive (2014) for implementation by all member states from June 2016 (EC 2017).

2016 – Directive (2014/56/EU) and Regulation (537/2014) become effective in June 2016:

> The new audit rules aim for better audit quality and a more competitive audit market for statutory audits of PIEs to enable capital markets to run smoothly (EC 2016). The new EU Audit Reform addresses several shortcomings observed in the audit market. First, deficiencies, and in some instances misstatements, have been detected in audit reports by Member States' competent authorities. Second, doubts had emerged amongst investors about the credibility and reliability of the audited financial statements of banks, other financial institutions, and listed companies, as highlighted by the GFC. This seriously dented the confidence of investors in the reports of statutory auditors. Third, an excessive familiarity between the management of a company and its audit firm, risks of conflicts of interest, and threats to the independence of statutory auditors, challenged the ability of statutory auditors to exert thorough professional scepticism. Fourth, there was a lack of choice of audit firms emanating from high concentration levels in the top end of the audit market. Finally, there was a systemic risk, as the audit market has been effectively dominated at the top end by four large firms, Deloitte, EY, KPMG, and PwC (EC 2016). The CEAOB began working in 2016 to improve cooperation between European national audit authorities in the EU. The CEAOB contributes to the proper application of EU audit legislation by facilitating supervisory convergence (EC 2017).

1.3 The EU Audit Reform 2014

According to a recent EU Parliament Report (2019), the EU Audit Reform 2014 came into being in the aftermath of the GFC. Its major aim was to strengthen confidence in the integrity of reported financial statements and improve audit quality. In achieving this goal, one of the main objectives of the EU Audit Reform 2014 was to make the top end of the audit market more dynamic (Girdhar and Jeppesen, 2018; Horton et al., 2018). In the aftermath of the GFC, significant weaknesses were identified in the statutory audit function, which were cited as a factor in auditors failing to provide any warning signals about troubled banks (see, e.g., Humphrey et al., 2009). This strong criticism started to raise concerns about the accuracy of audited financial statements of large companies, and intensified issues around auditor independence (EU Parliament Report, 2019).

Among other provisions, the EU Audit Reform 2014 established specific requirements regarding statutory audit of PIEs. The new rules followed an extensive consultation process, which started with the EU Commission's Green Paper on Audit Policy in October 2010 and resulted in the presentation of two Commission proposals in November 2011. However, as mentioned above, these two proposals found serious opposition and were extensively modified before the 2014 (final) version. However, as with many EU directives, there have been transposition and interpretation issues (Chatzivgeri et al., 2019). For instance, there are EU Member State differences in the definition of a PIE. Denmark, Sweden, and the UK follow the EU definition of a PIE, whereas Croatia, Spain, and Italy have definitions different from the EU definition (EU Parliament Report, 2019) at the national level. To be aligned with the EU Audit Reform (2014), the definition of PIEs has been extended in Germany, Slovenia, Sweden, and the UK. In Italy, the Legislation Decree 135/2016 implementing the EU Audit Reform (2014) introduced a new category of entities "Entity subject to an intermediate regulatory regime." This category is subject to the same regime as the PIE for auditor's independence.

The key changes included in the EU Audit Reform (2014) were the extended auditors' report, mandatory firm rotation by auditors, caps, bans, and restrictions on NAS, and more powers for audit committees. The stricter requirements that apply to the statutory audit of PIEs, based on the implementation of the EU Regulation (537/2014), are:

- Strengthening the requirements on the external audit report, and introducing an additional, more detailed report to the audit committee, containing thorough information about the performance of the external audit.
- Introducing a maximum ten-year firm rotation with the option for Member States to choose shorter periods (e.g., Italy opted for a nine-year mandatory audit firm rotation) for PIEs. A further 10 years can be added, up to a maximum of 20 years, where a public tendering process is conducted. For joint audit arrangements, a further 14 years is allowed, up to a maximum of 24 years (ICAEW, 2016).
- Establishing a list of NAS that cannot be provided by the statutory external auditor or audit firm to the audited entity. Limitations on the service fees charged for NAS are also imposed.
- Enhancing the role and competencies of the audit committee, giving it a prominent direct role in the appointment of the statutory external auditor, as well as in the monitoring of the audit process (FRC, 2007, 2009, 2010).

In summary, the extended audit report was introduced by regulators with two aims. The first aim is to provide a real focus on the issues that are being addressed in the external audit, with corresponding requirements for audit committees in relation to these issues. The second aim is to have the external auditors stating more information about the audit itself. In addition, the EU Audit Reform (2014) addresses auditor independence concerns through the introduction of mandatory rotation which, at the general level, can entail: (1) mandatory partner rotation; and (2) mandatory audit firm rotation. Such changes aim at increasing audit quality and may have impacts on external auditors' organisational and managerial practices. Audit committees of PIEs are now required to rotate external auditors periodically, though the period may vary across Member States. The general rule is that the external auditors must be rotated at least every ten years. However, Member States may choose to reduce this period to a shorter period or may also permit PIEs to continue with the incumbent external auditor for a maximum of 20 years if a transparent tender procedure has taken place, or for a maximum of 24 years if there have been joint audits.

The EU Regulation (537/2014) has also introduced specific restrictions on a range of NAS that PIEs in the EU can obtain from the audit firm and its network. The restrictions apply to the period between the beginning of the period audited and the issuing of the audit report, as well as to the financial year immediately preceding the period audited. The NAS that are prohibited by the EU reform are the following:

1 certain tax services.
2 services that involve playing any part in the management or decision-making of the audited entity.
3 bookkeeping and preparing accounting records and financial statements.
4 designing and implementing internal control or risk management procedures related to the preparation and/or control of financial information, or the design and implementation of financial information technology systems.
5 certain valuation services (e.g., performed in connection with actuarial or litigation support services).
6 certain legal services.
7 services related to the audited entity's internal audit function.
8 services linked to the financing, capital structure and allocation, and investment strategy, of the audited entity.
9 promoting, dealing in, or underwriting, shares in the audited entity.
10 payroll and other human resources services.

Member States may add to the list of prohibitions and may adopt legislation further restricting NAS, with one important exception: Member States may not set a lower threshold in relation to NAS prohibition. Finally, the EU Audit Reform (2014) assigns greater powers to the audit committee appointed by PIEs. There are two main changes: (1) related to audit firm selection and tenure; and (2) the additional written report the auditors provide to the client's audit committee.

1.4 Objectives of the research

The aim of the research is to undertake a comparative analysis of how the EU Audit Reform (2014) has impacted external financial statement auditors in the market for audit and assurance services in Europe, by comparing two very different European regulatory and cultural contexts: the UK and Italy. Evidence is still limited on the impacts of this EU Audit Reform on European auditors, especially with respect to the regulatory, economic, and cultural differences amongst European countries. The research in this book compares the differential impacts of these reforms on the managerial and organisational practices of larger and smaller audit practitioners in the UK and Italy. The UK and Italy are purposively selected as representing two very different institutional settings, which will offer insights on how the efforts of standardising audit regulation may lead to very different organisational responses within Europe. The comparison of different institutional settings is deemed useful for drawing relevant insights for policymakers and practitioners. By considering the views of external auditors and other key stakeholders, this research book will assist policymakers and professional accounting bodies in assessing the impact of regulatory interventions on external auditor behaviour and practice. Hence, the broad objective of the research is to address the following question:

> *How do the impacts on external auditors of the latest EU reforms to audit compare between the UK and Italy, and how have these regulatory reforms affected audit firms' practices and the future of audit in Europe?*

To address this research question, first, we compare the overall impacts of this EU Audit Reform between the UK and Italy and consider the perceptions of both larger and smaller audit practitioners in doing so. Second, we focus on how the EU reforms have impacted audit firms' organisational activities and audit practices, such as external audit processes and methodologies, audit strategies and policies, and risk management systems. To such an end, the UK and Italy offer a suitable setting because they represent two contrasting models of European regulatory, economic, and cultural background (Hofstede, 1984; Cooke and Wallace, 1990; Nobes, 1998). In addition, by considering non-Big Four auditors, we provide a more holistic view into the EU Audit Reform's impacts on external auditors, as non-Big Four firms are a significant part of the accounting profession (Houghton et al., 2010). To obtain a comprehensive picture of the impacts of the EU Audit Reform (2014), we also consider the perceptions of other subjects who interact with external auditors (e.g., audit clients, audit committee members, and directors), have the capability to affect their activity (e.g., regulators and professional bodies), and/or are affected by their activity (e.g., investors).

This research provides insights from auditors and other market players regarding their reactions to major reforms in the period after their implementation, and highlights some of the different concerns of the larger and smaller audit firms. By understanding the impacts of these latest audit provisions, this study provides insights into different responses to regulatory changes that have occurred among audit firms in two different European countries. As a result, this study can assist in addressing issues related to public policy work and in exploring challenges faced by key stakeholders in the market for audit and assurance services, in promoting audit quality, better communication about the role of the auditor, capital market stability and confidence, and auditor independence.

1.5 Research approach

Qualitative approaches are particularly well aligned with the nature of the above research question and the issues that need to be addressed. To help answer this research question, face-to-face semi-structured interviews and focus groups were conducted with auditors, financial market regulators, accounting standard setters, investors, staff from professional accounting bodies, and listed company directors involved with audit committees (together referred to as "stakeholders"). This wide range of participants helped in gathering opinions that reflect different perspectives on audit regulations and the profession, due to their different roles. The interviews and focus groups provided an opportunity to probe issues in more depth. These in-depth approaches provide a source of data richness, as the researchers can enquire further into the complexity of issues.

Focus groups and interviews were conducted in both major business cities and regional centres, such as Edinburgh, London, Milan, Rome, and Verona. Face-to-face semi-structured interviews were used for participants who could not join the allocated focus group times. The focus groups or office interviews, each lasting approximately two hours, were conducted throughout late 2017, 2018, and early 2019. When possible, focus groups and interviews were audio recorded to capture the detail of these discussions. In the two countries, in total 50 participants were involved during 2018 and 2019. To ensure quality control, at least two members of the research team were at every focus group run or interview for this research project in each of these cities reached. Thematic analysis was used to induce themes and draw conclusions that are developed from the analysis. The data collected were coded to identify dominant themes within the key stakeholder groups involved in this research. The dominant themes identified were compared to highlight similarities and differences between the two countries, the UK and Italy (Boyatzis, 1998). Table 1.1a indicates that 10 of the 23 UK participants are audit partners and 20 of the 23 UK participants are male. There is a slightly better spread of different stakeholder groups in the UK sample than in Italy. Table 1.1b conveys that, in Italy, 13 of the 23 participants are audit partners and 22 of the 27 participants are male. Table 1.1c indicates that the participants were predominately from London, Milan, and Verona.

Table 1.1a Summary of participants from the UK by stakeholder group (London and Edinburgh)

Categorisation	*N*
Regulators	3
Standard setters	1
Big Four audit partners	6
Non-Big Four audit partners	4
Audit committee chairs	2
Investors	2
Chief Financial Officers (CFOs)	1
Professional body members (staff)	4
Total	23
Gender	Males (20), females (3)

Table 1.1b Summary of participants from Italy by stakeholder group (Milan, Rome, and Verona)

Categorisation	*N*
Regulators	4
Big Four audit partners	8
Non-Big Four audit partners	5
Audit committee chairs or members of a Board of Statutory Auditors (BSA)	10
Total	27
Gender	Males (22), females (5)

Table 1.1c Summary of participants from the UK and Italy by stakeholder group and location (2018–2019)

Location >	*UK*		*Italy*		
	London	*Edinburgh*	*Verona*	*Rome*	*Milan*
Regulators	3	–	–	4	–
Standard setters	1	–	–	–	–
Big Four audit partners	5	1	6	–	2
Non-Big Four audit partners	4	–	2	–	3
Audit committee chairs/BSA	2	–	5	–	5
Investors	2	–	–	–	–
CFO (chief accountant)	–	1	–	–	–
Professional body members (staff)	3	1	–	–	–
Total	20	3	13	4	10

Transcribed audio recordings were coded into relevant research themes and analysed using NVivo, a computer-assisted qualitative data analysis software specifically designed for thematic analysis (Mills et al., 2009). Using the software, textual patterns were identified from the focus groups and interviews to detect trends and themes within the data to enable conclusions to be drawn in an organised manner. Table 1.2a and b contains background details on the 50 participants in the study. Table 1.2a indicates that the UK participants are predominately over the age of 55 (70%), and with over 15 years of experience in the accounting field (83%). Table 1.2b indicates that the Italian participants are of a younger demographic, mainly in the age range 46–55 (52%); however, most have over 15 years of experience in the accounting field (85%), as for the UK group.

Table 1.2a Background on all the UK participants (2018–2019)

Groups of respondents	*Number of respondents*	*Age*	*Years of experience*
Regulators	3 (2 males (m), 1 female(f))	46–55 years (f) (1) >55 years (m) (2)	>15 years (3)
Standard setters	1 (1 male)	>55 years (m) (1)	>30 years (1)
Audit partners with Big Four firms	6 (5 males, 1 female)	46–55 years (m, f) (2) >55 years (m) (4)	>15 years (6)
Audit partners with non-Big Four firms	4 (4 males)	>55 years (m) (4)	>15 years (4)
Chairs of Audit Committee listed FTSE companies	2 (2 males)	>55 years (m) (2)	>30 years (2)
Investors	2 (2 males)	>55 years (m) (2)	>15 years (2)
Professional body staff members	4 (3 males, 1 female)	34–45 years (m, f) (4)	10–14 years (4)
CFO	1 (1 male)	>55 years (m) (1)	>30 years (1)
Total	23		

Further research was conducted in 2022 which included an online survey of around 85 participants that work or used to work in the audit profession in Europe and the UK (with 49 fully completed surveys). The findings from the survey are analysed and discussed further in Chapters 7 and 8. The survey specifically focused on digital transformation within the audit profession and future challenges for external auditors.

Table 1.2b Background on all the Italian participants (2018–2019)

Groups of respondents	*Number of respondents*	*Age*	*Years of experience*
Financial market regulators	*4 (1 male (m), 3 female (f))*	*46–55 years (f) (1)* *>55 years (m, f) (3)*	*>15 years (1)* *>30 years (3)*
Audit partners with Big Four firms	8 (8 males)	36–45 years (m) (3) 46–55 years (m) (3) >55 years (m) (2)	10–14 years (3) >15 years (3) >30 years (2)
Audit partners with non-Big Four firms	5 (4 males, 1 female)	46–55 years (m, f) (5)	10–14 years (1) >15 years (3) >30 years (1)
Members of the Internal Control and Audit Committee	10 (9 males, 1 female)	36–45 years (m) (1) 46–55 years (m, f) (5) >55 years (m) (4)	>15 years (4) >30 years (6)
Total	27		

1.6 Outline of chapters

Chapter 2: Institutional setting and audit regulation in Europe

Keywords: Audit Reform, Audit Quality, Corporate Governance

Chapter 2 summarises institutional differences that characterise several European countries and opens discussion towards the analysis of the impacts of the EU Audit Reform (2014) in Chapters 3–8. Chapter 2 follows on from Chapter 1 by separately explaining how the EU Audit Directive (2014) has been applied in Europe. In Chapter 2, the institutional characteristics of several European countries are presented, with attention to their legal systems, their corporate governance systems, and their audit regulation and market. Issues around audit quality are then discussed with reference to relevant past research, reviews, and commissioned reports.

Chapter 3: New audit reports: improving informational content and value

Keywords: Auditor Reporting, Communication

Chapter 3 examines the effects of the information disclosed via the extended audit reports. As previous research emphasised, there is a need for enhancing the informative content and value of the audit product; thereby the new audit report has been intended to offer auditors an opportunity to give financial statement users some sense of what the audit looks like in terms of scope. This new generation of audit reports includes disclosures about significant matters in a company's financial reporting and its audit. These disclosures are a landmark change in auditors' responsibility to provide information to shareholders. These issues are further examined in this chapter.

Chapter 4: Mandatory auditor rotation: perceived benefits and costs

Keywords: Auditor Tenure, cooling-Off Periods

Chapter 4 contains an analysis of the impacts of the EU Audit Reform (2014) in relation to mandatory audit firm rotation, which was introduced to address auditor independence concerns. Audit committees of PIEs are now required to rotate auditors periodically, though the period may vary across Member States. The general rule is that the audit firms must be rotated at least every ten years. We provide an overview of prior regulations and literature on such a debated issue. Qualitative evidence is then offered on the perceived impacts of the EU Audit Reform (2014) on audit quality, on audit costs and audit fees, and on the concentration of the audit market.

Chapter 5: Restrictions and caps on non-audit work: challenges and response strategies

Keywords: Consulting Services, Other Non-audit Services

Chapter 5 analyses the impacts of the EU Audit Reform (2014) in relation to the use of restrictions and caps on NAS. Within this chapter we also examine and discuss issues related to the adjustments to internal quality controls within audit firms, audit processes and strategies, and recalibrations to audit firms' risk management systems and structures, in response to such changes. The EU Audit Reform (2014) has introduced specific restrictions on a range of NAS that PIEs in the EU can obtain from the audit firm and its network. The restrictions apply to the period between the beginning of the period audited and the issuing of the audit report, as well as to the financial year immediately preceding the period audited. These reforms are explained in more detail in Chapter 5.

Chapter 6: Audit committees: greater powers and proposed standards

Keywords: Corporate Governance, Board Oversight

Chapter 6 provides an overview of the evolution of the powers and roles of audit committees (AC) in Europe before and after the enactment of the EU Audit Reform (2014). It provides an overview of the main findings of studies that have investigated the effects of regulations on AC function and powers, with a particular focus on the EU Audit Reform (2014). Chapter 6 also analyses the key perceptions of auditors and regulators of the key impacts of the EU Audit Reform (2014) in terms of AC's powers and considers proposed standards for audit committees as this is now being considered in the UK.

Chapter 7: The future of audit: impacts of new technologies

Keywords: Automation, Data analytics, Standard Setting

Chapter 7 conveys that as new digital technologies in audit become more routine in audit practice, professional standards will need to evolve to address the challenges that these technologies currently present. Some emerging technologies, such as machine learning and predictive analysis, present further opportunities to improve audit quality but raise challenges for both audit firms and regulators in terms of compliance with standards. In Chapter 7 we share how emerging technologies have created what can be described as a digital revolution in audit, and how this has impacted the current audit business model. The revolution of technology is rapidly tackling various prospects in the field; however, there remains uncertainty about future outcomes. Results of an online survey conducted during 2022 are conveyed and analysed further in Chapter 7, focusing on the digital transformation within the audit profession.

Chapter 8: The new paths of statutory audits in Europe: meeting public expectations and other future challenges

Keywords: Expectation's Gap, Future Challenges

This final chapter conveys the challenges as perceived by the audit profession within the next five years. This chapter also highlights what the future of auditing might look like in the EU, particularly after Brexit and considering changes to regulatory frameworks that might be required to help meet public expectations. Questions have been raised as to whether the existing assurance framework remains fit for purpose in the 21st century. Auditors will be increasingly asked to provide assurance over information that is more subjective in nature and time will tell if the existing levels of assurance will continue to meet the needs of users. What has been known for decades as the "audit expectations gap" is explained in this final chapter and discussed further. Future challenges are considered such as retaining the best and brightest graduate auditors, the risks of more regulatory intervention in the audit and assurance services market and issues that impact smaller practitioners differently than the Big Four audit firms, such as Deloitte, EY, KPMG, and PwC. Results of an online survey conducted during 2022 are conveyed and analysed further in Chapter 8, focusing on the future of audit and the challenges those external auditors face in the future.

References

Boyatzis, R. (1998). *Transforming qualitative information: Thematic analysis and code development*. Thousand Oaks, CA: Sage Publications, Inc.

Chatzivgeri, E., Chew, L., Crawford, L., Gordon, M., and Haslam, J. (2019). Transparency and accountability for the global good? The U.K.'s implementation of EU law requiring country-by-country reporting of payments to governments by extractives. *Critical Perspectives in Accounting*. https://doi.org/10.1016/j.cpa.2019.02.001

Cooke, T.E., and Wallace, R.O. (1990). Financial disclosure regulation and its environment: A review and further analysis. *Journal of Accounting and Public Policy*, 9(2): 79–110.

DG (2003). Modernising company law and enhancing corporate governance in the European Union – A plan to move forward. 284 final of 21 May 2003. Available at: http://www.ecgi.org/commission/documents/governance_consult_responses_en.pdf. Accessed 08.04.19.

European Commission (2000). Consultative paper on statutory auditors' independence in the EU: A set of fundamental principles. https://eur-lex.europa.eu/legal-content/EN/TXT/?uri=CELEX:32002H0590. Accessed 25.11.22.

European Commission (2010). Green Paper – Audit policy: Lessons from the crisis. Available at: http://eur-lex.europa.eu/legal-content/EN/TXT/PDF/?uri=-CELEX:52010DC0561&from=EN. Accessed 18.02.19.

European Commission (2016). Reform of the EU Statutory Audit Market. Available at: http://europa.eu/rapid/press-release_MEMO-16-2244_en.htm. Accessed 03.03.19.

European Commission (2017). Report on monitoring developments in the EU market for providing statutory audit services to public-interest entities pursuant to Article 27 of Regulation (EU) 537/2014. Available at: https://eur-lex.europa.eu/legal-content/EN/TXT/PDF/?uri=CELEX:52017DC0464&from=EN. Accessed 04.03.19.

European Union (EU) (2014a). Directive 2006/43/EC of the European Parliament and of the Council of 17 May 2006 on statutory audits of annual accounts and consolidated accounts. Available at: https://eur-lex.europa.eu/legal-content/EN/TXT/HTML/?uri=CELEX:32014L0056&from=EN. Accessed 15.03.19.

European Union (EU) (2014b). Regulation (EU) No 537/2014 of the European parliament and of the council of 16 April 2014 on specific requirements regarding statutory audit of public-interest entities and repealing Commission Decision 2005/909/EC. Available at: http://eur-lex.europa.eu/legal-content/EN/TXT/PDF/?uri=CELEX:32014R0537&from=EN. Accessed 15.03.19.

European Union Parliament Report (2019). EU Statutory Audit Reform: Impact on costs, concentration, and competition. By Willekens, M., Dekeyser, S., and Simac I., PE 631.057. Available at: http://www.europarl.europa.eu/RegData/etudes/STUD/2019/631057/IPOL_STU(2019)631057_EN.pdf. Accessed 22.04.2019.

Financial Reporting Council—FRC (2007). Choice in the UK Audit market final report of the market participants group. Available at: https://www.frc.org.uk/Our-Work/Publications/FRC-Board/Final-report-of-the-Market-Participants-Group-200.pdf. Accessed 18.03.19.

Financial Reporting Council—FRC (2009). Choice in the UK Audit market – Third progress report. Available at: https://www.frc.org.uk/Our-Work/Publications/FRC-Board/Choice-in-the-UK-Audit-Market-Third-Progress-Repor.pdf. Accessed 24.03.19.

Financial Reporting Council—FRC (2010). Submission to the House of Lords economic affairs committee: "Auditors: Market Concentration and their Role". Available at: https://www.frc.org.uk/Our-Work/Publications/FRC-Board/Choice-FRC-submission-to-HOL-Inquiry.pdf. Accessed 28.04.19.

Girdhar, S., and Jeppesen, K. (2018). Practice variation in Big 4 transparency reports. *Accounting, Auditing and Accountability Journal*, 31(1): 261–285.

Hofstede, G. (1984). *Culture's consequences: International differences in work-related values* (Vol. 5). London: Sage.

Horton, J., Tsipouridou, M., and Wood, A. (2018). European market reaction to audit reforms. *European Accounting Review,* 27(5): 991–2013.

Houghton, K., Jubb, C., Kend, M., and Ng, J. (2010). *The future of audit: Keeping capital markets efficient.* Canberra: ANU Press.

Humphrey, C., Loft, A., and Woods, M. (2009). The global audit profession and the international financial architecture: Understanding regulatory relationships at a time of financial crisis. *Accounting, Organizations and Society,* 34: 810–825.

Institute of Chartered Accountants of England and Wales—ICAEW (2016). Implementation of European audit reforms. Available at: http://www.icaew.com/en/technical/ethics/auditor-independence/implementation-of-european-audit-reforms. Accessed 14.03.19.

International Monetary Fund (2018). *World economic outlook report: Challenges to steady growth,* October 2018.

Kend, M., and Basioudis, I.G. (2018). Reforms to the market for audit and assurance services in the period after the global financial crisis: Evidence from the UK. *Australian Accounting Review,* 28(4): 589–597.

Law 262/2005. Legge 28 dicembre 2005, n. 262 – "Disposizioni per la tutela del risparmio e la disciplina dei mercati finanziari". Available at: https://www.camera.it/parlam/leggi/05262l.htm. Accessed 12.09.2019.

Legislative Decree 303/2006. Decreto Legislativo 29 dicembre 2006, n. 303 – "Coordinamento con la legge 28 dicembre 2005, n. 262, del testo unico delle leggi in materia bancaria e creditizia (T.U.B.) e del testo unico delle disposizioni in materia di intermediazione finanziaria (T.U.F.)". Available at: https://www.camera.it/parlam/leggi/deleghe/06303dl.htm. Accessed 02.07.2019.

Legislative Decree 39/2010. Decreto Legislativo 27 gennaio 2010, n. 39 – "Attuazione della direttiva 2006/43/CE, relativa alle revisioni legali dei conti annuali e dei conti consolidati, che modifica le direttive 78/660/CEE e 83/349/CEE, e che abroga la direttiva 84/253/CEE". Available at: https://www.camera.it/parlam/leggi/deleghe/10039dl.htm. Accessed 15.02.2020.

Maijoor, S., and Vanstraelen, A. (2012). Research opportunities in auditing in the EU – revisited. *Auditing: A Journal of Practice and Theory,* 31(1): 115–126.

Marriage, M. (2018). Grant Thornton exits audit market for big UK companies. *Financial Times,* 29 March.

Mills, A., Durepos, G., and Wiebe, E. (2009). *Encyclopedia of case study research.* London: Sage Publications.

Needles Jr, B.E. (1989). International auditing research: Current assessment and future direction. *The International Journal of Accounting,* 24(1): 1–20.

Nobes, C. (1998) Towards a general model of the reasons for international differences in financial reporting. *ABACUS: A Journal of Accounting, Finance and Business Studies,* 34(2): 162–187.

Ratzinger-Sakel, N.V.S., and Schönberger, M.W. (2015). Restricting non-audit services in Europe – The potential (lack of) impact of a blacklist and a fee cap on auditor independence and audit quality. *Accounting in Europe,* 12(1): 61–86.

Schilder, A. (1996). Research opportunities in auditing in the European Union. *Accounting Horizons,* 10(4): 98–108.

Stevenson, J.E. (2002). Auditor independence: A comparative descriptive study of the U.K., France, and Italy. *International Journal of Auditing,* 6(2): 155–182.

2 Institutional setting and audit regulation in Europe

2.1 Introduction

In the past decades, several successive EU (European Union) Directives have regulated accounting standards, auditing, and corporate governance to harmonise these practices throughout the EU. However, the process of harmonisation is often difficult to achieve because of the significant differences that characterise countries across the EU. Indeed, European countries have institutional and cultural differences that may affect how such implementation takes place. For instance, continental Europe (e.g., Belgium, France, Germany, Italy, and Spain) is dominated by national Commercial Codes related to corporate and tax legislation, which are the backbone to accounting standardisation (Niyama, 2010); however, these are implemented differently due to institutional and cultural differences between these countries.

In the following sections, the institutional characteristics of European countries are presented, with attention to their legal systems, their corporate governance systems, and their audit regulation and market. Table 2.1 summarises these differences between four countries: Germany, the UK, France, and Italy.

2.2 Legal systems

Legal systems of countries around the world generally fall into two main categories: common law and civil law. Common law countries are typically those that were former British colonies whilst countries following a civil law system are typically those that were former French, Dutch, German, Spanish, or Portuguese colonies. In Europe, only four countries can be classified as common law. These are Cyprus, Gibraltar, Ireland, and the UK. All the remaining European countries have a national legal system based on civil law.

A common law environment is characterised by the lack of a written constitution or codified laws. It offers a high degree of protection to creditors and shareholders (La Porta et al., 1998), higher transparency (La Porta

DOI: 10.4324/9781003262596-2

Table 2.1 Summary of the main differences in the legal systems, corporate governance, audit regulation, and audit market in the four largest European countries, by GDP: Germany, the UK, France, and Italy

	Germany	*UK*	*France*	*Italy*
Legal system	**Civil law** Main sources of regulation on corporate governance are the German Stock Corporation Act and the German Limited Liability Corporate. Additional recommendations are set by the German Corporate Governance Code. German listed companies are required to use EU-adopted IFRS. Private companies follow the accounting standards set by the German Commercial Code (Handelsgesetzbuch).	**Common law** The accountancy profession and institutional investors are trend-setters in corporate governance practices. Corporate governance is mostly regulated with voluntary recommendations set up by the UK. Code of Corporate Governance (FRC 2016). Accounting is regulated according to the rules issued by the FRC. UK listed companies are required to use UK-adopted IFRS.	**Civil law** The main source of corporate governance regulation is the French Commercial Code. Additional recommendations are set in the Afep-Medef Corporate Governance Code. French listed companies are required to use EU-adopted IFRS. Accounting standards for private companies are set by the ANC.	**Civil law** Regulation on corporate governance originates from the Italian Company Law and is included in the Italian Civil Code. Additional recommendations are set by the Italian Corporate Governance Code. Italian listed companies are required to use EU-adopted IFRS. Accounting standards for unlisted companies are set by the Organismo Italiano di Contabilità.

(*Continued*)

	Germany	*UK*	*France*	*Italy*
Corporate governance system	**Germanic** Companies listed in Germanic countries usually have one or a few large shareholders that control them. Stakeholder-oriented. Dominant shareholders, employees, and banks are the most influential stakeholders. Two-tier board of directors, which comprises a management board and a supervisory board. Stock markets play a less important role than in Anglo-Saxon countries. Active market for corporate control is almost inexistent, and very few hostile takeovers take place.	**Anglo-Saxon** High degree of separation between ownership and control. Main agency problem is between managers and shareholders. Shareholder-oriented. Institutional investors are the most influential stakeholders. One-tier board of directors, characterised by the presence of executive and non-executive directors that are members of the same board. Stock markets and the external market for corporate control are very active.	**Latin** High degree of concentration between ownership and control. Main agency problem is between dominant and minority shareholders. Firms are usually characterised by the presence of a dominant shareholder (usually a family, a bank, or another corporation). Institutional investors or banks have small or no influence on companies' governance. Companies can choose between one-tier or two-tier board systems. Most of the companies choose the one-tier system. Stock markets are less developed than in Anglo-Saxon countries, but more developed than in the other Latin countries. No active market for corporate control exists.	**Latin** High degree of concentration between ownership and control. Main agency problem is between dominant and minority shareholders. Firms are usually characterised by the presence of a dominant shareholder (usually a family, a bank, or another corporation). Institutional investors or banks have small or no influence on companies' governance. Companies can choose between one-tier, two-tier, or the traditional Italian board system. Most companies use the traditional system, which consists of a board of directors and a board of statutory auditors. Stock markets and the external market for corporate control are not well developed and active.

	Germany	UK	France	Italy
Audit regulation	Audit regulation is contained in the German Commercial Code. Additional guidance on audit is provided by the Institut der Wirtschaftsprüfer (Institute of Auditors), in line with the EU regulation. A ten-year mandatory audit firm rotation has been introduced as the results of the EU audit reform. Further restrictions on the nature and extent of NAS that auditors can provide to PIEs were also introduced after the Audit EU legislation. The provision of certain tax services and valuation service as NAS is allowed.	Audit regulation is set out by the Companies Act 2006 and various domestic codes and regulations, which reflect the EU legislative framework. The FRC is the key actor in setting audit regulation. It requires ten-year mandatory audit firm rotation (since 2015). It also requires (since 2009) the rotation of the audit engagement partner (after five years) the engagement quality control review partner (after seven years) and other key audit partners (after seven years).	Auditing requirements are in line with the EU regulation. Auditing standards are prepared by the Compagnie nationale des commissaires aux comptes (CNCC) and the High Council for Statutory Audits (H3C). France is one of the few countries in the world that mandates companies with consolidated accounts to be audited by at least two auditing firms (joint audit). France is the only country in Europe that implemented the disclosure on the KAMs before it was mandated by the IAASB. Ten-year mandatory audit firm rotation was introduced as the result of the 2014 Audit EU legislation.	Auditing requirements are transposed by EU regulations. Audit is overseenby the MEF and the Commissione Nazionale per le Società e la Borsa (CONSOB). Italy was one of the first countries in the world to mandate audit firm rotation (since 1975). Since 2010, audit firm rotation has been compulsory every nine years. Audit partner rotation is mandatory every seven years. These provisions remain unchanged after the introduction of the audit reform in 2016. Regulation on NAS was also in place before the audit reform. The list of prohibited NAS activities has been enlarged as the result of the Audit EU legislation. Italy's reliance on the EU regulation for NAS restrictions is without any exception.

(Continued)

	Germany	*UK*	*France*	*Italy*
	NAS fee caps were introduced as the result of the EU audit reform. Companies are simply required to disclose the total fees for the services provided by the audit firm.	Restrictions to NAS were introduced since 2010. A NAS regulations exists next to the EU regulation. The provision of certain tax services and valuation service as NAS is allowed. NAS fee caps were introduced as the result of the Audit EU legislation. Companies are required to disclose in their annual reports audit fees. Separate disclosure is needed for other type of service provided.	Regulation on NAS was very restrictive even before the Audit Directive: auditors can only perform audit and audit-related services for the firms they audit. France reliance on the EU regulation for NAS restrictions is without any exception. NAS fee caps were introduced as the result of the Audit EU legislation Listed companies in France are mandated to separately disclose audit and non-audit fees. Audit fees need to be split in actual audit fees, and fees directly related to the audit.	NAS fee caps were introduced as the result of the Audit EU legislation. Italian listed companies are required to disclose the audit fees and the NAS activities and fees in their annual reports.

	Germany	*UK*	*France*	*Italy*
Audit market	The audit market consists of 1,040 statutory audits of PIEs. Big Four audited 91% of the 160 largest listed companies in Germany. Germany has the second largest market share in Europe in terms of turnover of audit firms auditing PIEs.	The audit market consists of 1,748 statutory audits of PIEs. 97% of audits of FTSE 350 companies are undertaken by the Big Four auditors. The UK has the largest market share in Europe in terms of turnover of audit firms auditing PIEs.	The audit market consists of 3,471 statutory audits of PIEs. This is because France requires joint audit. France has the majority of Joint PIEs' audit in EU (86% of total for the EU-28). Big Four companies account for just 57% of the overall market share among the largest listed companies.	The audit market consists of 1,578 statutory audits of PIEs The Big Four account for 98% of the audit market share. The remaining 2% were audited by BDO, the only non-Big Four company. Big Four's revenues collected from audit services provided to PIEs count as 18% of total revenue.

et al., 1999; Meek and Thomas, 2004), and a court system able to interpret and enforce commercial contracts because of common law principles (Keasey et al., 2005). The UK represents the best example of a common law system. British financial regulators, such as the Financial Reporting Council (FRC), the accountancy profession (e.g., ACCA, CIMA, ICAEW, ICAS), and institutional investors, have been considered as trend-setters in corporate governance practices that have been spread all over the world (Aguilera and Cuervo-Cazurra, 2003). The UK was the first country in the world to adopt a Corporate Governance Code, the Cadbury Report, in 1992, which seems to have been used as a model to follow by other countries worldwide in the development of their Corporate Governance Codes (Mallin, 2016). UK firms are regarded as having the best practices in Europe (Ferrarini et al., 2010). The UK accounting system is exemplified by flexibility and reliance on professional bodies, less conservatism, and higher transparency (Gray, 1988; Burgstahler et al., 2006). Accounting is regulated according to the rules issued by the FRC and the UK Companies Act (2006), apart from the consolidated financial statements of UK listed companies that have been subjected to IAS/IFRS International Financial Reporting Standards (IAS/IFRS) since 2005, when EC Regulation 1606/2002 ("the IAS Regulation") came into effect.

Civil law systems are a codified system of law based on the principle of Roman law, with a tradition of imposed legal compliance (La Porta et al., 1999; Meek and Thomas, 2004), including in the areas of corporate governance and accounting. They are based on a written constitution based on specific codes. Legislation is the primary source of law; only legislative enactments are considered binding for all. A civil law system is generally more prescriptive than a common law system. All the European countries except for Cyprus, Gibraltar, Ireland, the UK operate within a civil law system. France, Germany, and Italy represent good examples of civil law systems in Europe. In most of the countries that belong to the civil law system, accounting practices are regulated according to a rules-based system, where rules are released via decrees. In Germany, the main sources of regulation regarding corporate governance are the German Stock Corporation Act (Aktiengesetz – AktG), which deals with public companies, and the German Limited Liability Corporate Act (Gesetz betreffend die Gesellschaften mit beschränkterHaftung – GmbHG), which deals with private limited companies. In Italy, regulation regarding corporate governance originates from the Italian Company Law (Legislative Decree 6/2003) and is included in the Italian Civil Code. In France the main source of corporate governance regulation is the French Commercial Code, which provides rules covering the composition, powers, remuneration, duties and liabilities of the governing organs of companies. In addition, in most of the European civil law countries, additional sources of corporate governance regulation are provided by national Corporate Governance Codes, which adopts a "comply or explain" approach, whereby companies are invited to follow the guidelines or explain why they do not. These Corporate Governance Codes have been developed as based somewhat on the UK Corporate Governance Code published in 1992. France, Spain, and the Netherlands were among the first civil law countries in Europe to adopt a national Corporate Governance Code, respectively, in 1995, 1996, and 1997. Germany was among the last Western European civil law countries to adopt a Corporate Governance Code in 2000 (ECGI, n.d.). As for the other countries member of the EU, companies listed in EU civil law countries are required to adopt IAS/IFRS accounting standards for preparing the consolidated financial statement, because of the EC Regulation 1606/2002.[1] Unlisted companies are usually required to prepare their financial statements by using national accounting standards which are set by national bodies. For example, German accounting standards are set by the German Commercial Code (Handelsgesetzbuch), the French accounting standards by the Autorité des normes comptables (ANC), whereas the Italian accounting standards are set by the Organismo Italiano di Contabilità (Law 116/2014). These national accounting standards present similarities with the IAS/IFRS, but also important differences, which mostly relate to the use of fair value versus historical cost accounting and the other comprehensive income.[2]

2.3 Corporate governance systems

According to the predominant corporate governance literature (see, for example, De Jong, 1989; Weimer and Pape, 1999), European countries can be classified within three main corporate governance systems: Anglo-Saxon (the UK), Germanic (Austria, Denmark, Finland, Germany, Norway, Sweden, Switzerland, and the Netherlands), and Latin (Belgium, France, Italy, and Spain).

The Anglo-Saxon corporate governance system is characterised by a relatively high degree of separation between ownership and control, where firms usually lack a dominant shareholder (Mallin, 2016). The main purpose of corporation is to create value for shareholders. Corporate governance regulation is designed to mitigate the agency problems arising from this separation between ownership and control, with managers acting opportunistically to pursue self-serving interests at the expense of those of shareholders (Jensen and Meckling, 1976). The Anglo-Saxon corporate governance system operates based on soft regulation. The power and responsibilities to monitor the management of companies is in the hands of a one-tier board of directors which is appointed and dismissed by the shareholders at the general assembly. A one-tier board of directors is characterised by the presence of an appropriate combination of executive (inside) and non-executive (outside) directors that are members of the same board (FRC, 2018). Both executive and non-executive directors are responsible for the management of the firm and their accountability is primarily to shareholders (Lorsch and MacIver, 1989). Non-executive directors are usually considered to be outside experts and independent from the executive management of the firm (FRC, 2018). The idea is that non-executive directors, led by a senior independent director, should act as advisors on major policy decisions to executive directors and have the power to effectively monitor the management of the company, reducing the pursuit of their self-interest and ensuring that they act in the best interests of shareholders (Mallin, 2016). Stock markets and the external market for corporate control play a key role in the Anglo-Saxon system. The market for corporate control represents an additional control mechanism by means of which the stock market disciplines firms and promotes corporate efficiency, allowing control to be transferred from inefficient to efficient management teams (Keasey et al., 1997). The increasing economic dominance of capital markets, finance, and financial institutions (Davis and Kim, 2015), characterised by an increasing turnover of shares, has encouraged shareholders to focus on short-term goals at the expense of long-term sustainable development. In the UK, institutional investors have been criticised for their passivity and lack of interest in the oversight of the companies (Goergen and Renneboog, 2001; Tilba and McNulty, 2012). To encourage institutional investors to engage with the companies in which they invest, the FRC issued the first UK Stewardship Code in 2010, then revised this in 2012, with the aim of promoting the long-term success of companies in such a way that capital providers will also prosper (FRC, 2012).

The Germanic corporate governance system characterises most of the countries in continental Europe, such as Austria, Denmark, Finland, Germany, Norway, Sweden, Switzerland, and the Netherlands. In the Germanic system, the main aim of companies is not only, as in the Anglo-Saxon system, to create value for investors, but to guarantee value for all the stakeholders (Moerland, 1995; Goergen et al., 2008). Three groups of stakeholders are powerful and influential in the Germanic system: dominant shareholders, employees, and banks. Companies listed in Germanic countries usually have one or a few large shareholders that control them. They are subject to employee co-determination which gives employees the right to participate in the decision-making process of a corporation (Weimer and Pape, 1999). Companies are managed by a two-tier board of directors, which comprises a management board and a supervisory board. This structure guarantees a complete separation between those who manage the firm and those who supervise the management. The supervisory board is in charge to monitor the management board, and to provide advice on major[3] decisions. The composition of the supervisory board is determined not only by the shareholders, but also by the employees. The management board is appointed and dismissed by the supervisory board, which oversees the performance review of the management board. Another typical feature of the Germanic corporate governance system is the key role that banks play in the governance of firms as influential stakeholders (Weimer and Pape, 1999; Goergen et al., 2008). Banks influence the management of companies, by means of their position as equity owners and creditors (Baums, 1992). Together with families and other companies, banks are dominant shareholders of firms listed in Germanic countries. They also provide most of the debt capital of corporations which gives them access to insider information and the power of being represented on[4] supervisory boards (Hackethal et al., 2005). In Germanic countries, stock markets play a less important role than in Anglo-Saxon countries, and an active market for corporate control is almost inexistent, with very few hostile takeovers taking place (Hackethal et al., 2005).

The Latin corporate governance system presents features that are in between the Anglo-Saxon and the Germanic systems, but that are more like the latter. In Latin countries the stock market is not as developed as in Anglo-Saxon countries, with a few and slowly increasing number of publicly listed companies, which are strongly dependent on the banking system (Zingales, 1994; Zattoni, 1999; Bonacchi et al., 2018). However, while this is true for Italy and Spain, France presents a relatively well-developed stock market. A recent study of the OECD (2021) shows that, at the end of 2020, France was the second country in Europe with regard to market capitalisation (2,870,369 USD mil), after the UK (3,195,019 USD mil), but way above Germany (2,421,821 USD mil), Switzerland (1,933,137 USD mil), and the Netherlands (1,110,264 USD mil). While Italy, Spain, and Belgium occupied the seventh (730,529, USD mil), eighth (686,833 USD mil), and tenth positions, respectively (347,993 USD mil). As for Germanic countries, in Latin countries there is no active market for corporate control. The Latin system is also characterised by a high degree of concentration between ownership and control, where firms are usually characterised by the presence of a dominant shareholder which is usually a family, a bank, or another corporation (Weimer and Pape, 1999; Melis and Zattoni, 2017). Concentrated and family-owned ownership results in agency problems between controlling and outside shareholders. Controlling shareholders are usually able to have a direct control over the board of directors, by appointing themselves or professional executives close to them to board positions. As a result, agency problems are limited between executive directors and controlling shareholders; however, agency issues arise between the controlling and minority shareholders (Melis, 2000; Aguilera, 2005; Ben-Nasr et al., 2015). The protection of minority shareholders and investors is thus low in Latin countries (LaPorta et al., 1998; Enriques and Volpin, 2007). Moreover, institutional investors or banks have small or no influence on companies' governance (La Porta et al., 2000). In terms of board structure, in Latin countries, such as Italy and France, companies have the choice of using different board systems, whereas Spanish regulations require listed companies to adopted a one-tier board system. In France, companies can choose between a one-tier or a-tier board systems, with most of the companies choosing the unitary system (Millet-Reyes and Zhao, 2010). In Italy, the Italian Company Law provides companies with the opportunity to choose between three board systems: one-tier, two-tier, or the traditional

Italian board system, with many companies using the traditional system (Melis and Zattoni, 2017). The traditional Italian board system presents similarities with the one-tier system. It is characterised by the presence of a board of directors composed of executive and non-executive directors, which is responsible for the management of the business and is appointed and dismissed by the assembly of shareholders. However, unlike the one-tier system, it also includes an additional body: the *Collegio Sindacale* (Board of Statutory Auditors), an independent board appointed by shareholders, to supervise the board of directors and increase the minority shareholders' protection (Melis and Rombi, 2018). In part to limit the principal-principal agency problem, specific regulations are in place in some Latin countries to discipline the composition of the board of directors. For example, in Italy, national law grants minority shareholders the right to appoint at least one member of the board of directors (OECD, 2012). Since June 2007, all Italian listed firms are required to elect their board of directors by using the slate vote system. According to this system, at least one member of the board of directors must be elected from the minority slate that receives the largest number of votes and that is not linked in any way with the controlling shareholder's slate.

2.4 Audit regulation and audit market

This paragraph will provide an overview of the characteristics of the audit regulation and the audit market in Europe, by focusing on the four largest European countries by gross domestic product (GDP): Germany, the UK, France, and Italy.

2.4.1 Germany

Audit regulation in Germany is contained in the German Commercial Code (HGB) and extensive guidance on audit matters is provided by the Institut der Wirtschaftsprüfer (Institute of Auditors), which leads the auditing profession in Germany. According to this regulation, only qualified auditors are permitted to act as auditors for companies that are required by law to publish their financial statements. German auditors are required to prepare detailed reports for the management and supervisory boards where they need to comment on: (i) the scope, extent, and results of the audit process and (ii) management's evaluation of the financial position of the company as reported in the directors' report.

As the results of the transposition of the EU Audit Reform (2014), new audit requirements were implemented in Germany in 2016. These changes are mostly related to public interest entities (PIEs). According to the new regulation, audit in PIEs is characterised by a ten-year mandatory audit firm rotation. For non-financial-services PIEs, this period can be extended for a further 10 years following a tender process, and for further 14 years, if the incumbent auditor enters a joint audit. Germany was one of the EU countries that strongly opposed the introduction of mandatory audit firm rotation. Before the implementation of the requirements of the EU Audit Reform (2014), Germany adopted a mandatory seven-year audit partner rotation, rather than an audit firm rotation, as a measure to enhance audit quality. The new regulation also includes further restrictions on the nature and extent of non-audit services (NAS) that auditors can provide to PIEs (EU Audit Reforms 2014a, 2014b). According to the HGB, "a professional accountant cannot be the auditor if there are circumstances that might call auditor independence into question" (HCB, Paragraph 319), as in the following cases: participation in bookkeeping and preparation of the financial statements; participation in internal auditing in a responsible position; provision of financial or management services; provision of actuarial or valuation services that have a material impact on the financial statements (Hohenfels and Quick, 2020). For PIE clients, additional NAS, listed in the EU blacklist, are prohibited. These include the design and implementation of internal control/risk management procedures related to the preparation and/or control of financial information, payroll services, and certain human resource services. The provision of certain tax services and valuation services is allowed when they are immaterial and have no direct impact on the financial statements. As imposed by the EU regulation, in Germany NAS fees are capped at 70% of audit fees (based on a three-year average). The disclosure requirements in relation to audit fees in Germany are not very stringent. According to the Statutory Audit Directive of 2006, companies are simply required to disclose the total fees for the services provided by the audit firm. These can include fees for audit services, other assurance services, taxation services, and other services (Ratzinger-Sakel and Schönberger, 2015).

The German audit market consists of 1,040 statutory audits of PIEs (European Commission, 2017) and 73 registered audit firms auditing PIEs. In 2019, the Big Four audited 91% of the 160 largest listed companies in Germany (those belonging in the DAX 30, MDAX 60, and SDAX 70). KPMG was the leading auditor, with 51 companies, followed by PwC, with 46, EY, with 31, and Deloitte, with 17 (Audit Analytics, 2020a). Germany has the second largest market share in Europe in terms of turnover of audit firms auditing PIEs (with 5.7 EUR bil).

2.4.2 *The UK*

Historically, the FRC, and indeed the UK, has tended to lead the way in seeking to shape and adopt audit reforms and policy in Europe. Audit is a highly regulated activity, and clarity on audit regulation is very important for financial and audit markets. The FRC and the UK have been very influential at the European Commission when discussions have involved EU reforms to audit markets. Specifically, the FRC carries out regular reviews of audit regulation as well as inspections of auditors. In addition, it annually prepares and publishes an audit quality report regarding the quality of the services in the UK audit market. The audit legal requirements are set out by the Companies Act (2006) and various domestic codes and regulations which reflect elements of the European legislative framework. UK audit laws are substantially meant to be a direct translation of the EU Audit Reform (2014).

With reference to such regulation, the UK, after having already adopted partner rotation requirements in the past, follows the EU mandatory audit firm rotation requirements. It mandates audit firm rotation after ten years of continuous service, with the possibility of extending further ten years with the use of tendering (flexible implementation). The UK implemented the mandatory firm rotation rule from 1 January 2015, and this runs alongside the current audit and review partner rotation rules. Since 2009 in the UK, the audit engagement partner has had a maximum rotation period of five years, with a minimum five-year cooling-off period. However, flexibility of up to an additional two years is permitted where the audit committee believes that this is necessary to maintain audit quality, and such an extension is disclosed to shareholders. The engagement quality control review partner has had, since 2009, a maximum rotation period extended from five to seven years, with a cooling-off period of five years. Finally, other key audit partners have a maximum rotation period of seven years, with a two-year cooling-off period. The UK has experienced some restrictions to NAS that can be provided to the audit client since 2010 (Ratzinger-Sakel and Schönberger, 2015). It has an additional NAS regulation next to the EU regulation. As in Germany, the provision of certain tax services and valuation services, such as NAS, is allowed when they are immaterial and have no direct impact on the financial statements (EU Parliament Report, 2019). The UK is completely new to the restrictions on time frame and to fee caps as required by the EU Audit Reform (2014). Firms listed in the UK are required to disclose in their annual reports audit fees and separate disclosure is needed for other type of service provided (Ratzinger-Sakel and Schönberger, 2015).

The new UK regulatory body, the Audit, Reporting and Governance Authority (ARGA), which is expected to replace the FRC by 2025, will need to ensure that it will continue to lead the way on the global stage and have impact and influence over the remaining EU Member States and audit reforms, although Brexit is likely to impact that potential influence. The audit market in the UK consists of 1,748 statutory audits of PIEs (European Commission, 2017), with 97% of audits of FTSE 350 companies (the top end of the listed companies) undertaken by the Big Four auditors. Since 2014, the share of the Big Four in the entire London Stock Exchange has remained around 78% of the market by client count (EU Commission Report 2017; CMA, 2018). The UK has the largest market share in Europe in terms of turnover of audit firms auditing PIEs (with 15.3 EUR bil).

2.4.3 France

In France, the appointment of auditors in limited companies was made compulsory by the 1867 Act.[5] Since then, French regulation on audit has been modified several times, and four main provisions have been introduced to strengthen auditors' independence: joint audit, the identification of incompatibilities with carrying out auditors' assignments, the prohibition of auditors' involvement in management decisions, and audit rotation (Dattin, 2017). Since 1966, French regulation has imposed that companies with consolidated accounts be audited by at least two auditing firms. The presence of this joint audit requirement was as a valid alternative to the mandatory rotation of audit firms, which was introduced in France only after the implementation of the EU Audit Reform (2014). According to the current regulation, audit firms should rotate after an engagement period of ten years. Companies may, however, extend this period to a further 14 years, if there is a joint audit, and to further 6 years, with the use of tendering if there is no joint audit. The French regulation has also included a four-year cooling-off period during which a firm cannot be re-appointed. The mandate of audit firms' rotation was proposed and discussed by French regulators in 1998, many years before the enactment of the EU Audit Reform (2014). The proposal was however withdrawn as it was believed that it would have reduced audit quality. Instead, a six-year mandatory rotation of the audit partner was introduced by the 2003 Financial Safety Act.

The same Act also introduced a disclosure requirement like the "Key Audit Matters" (KAMs), called Justification of Assessments, long before these were regulated by the International Auditing and Assurance Standards Board (IAASB). The introduction of KAMs is one of the most significant changes to the audit reporting model in the past 90 years (Coram and Wang, 2020). The purpose of KAMs is to disclose financial reporting risks, thereby enhancing the communication value of the external audit report. KAMs are financial reporting matters that, in the external auditor's professional judgement, require significant auditor attention during the statutory audit (ASA 701/ISA 701). Some academic researchers consider that the new audit reporting requirements are likely to increase auditors' accountability, which should result in improved audit quality (IAASB, 2013; Peecher et al., 2013). Others suggest that the new audit reporting requirements may impose additional pressure on external auditors and thus have an adverse effect on audit quality (KPMG, 2015). France is the only country in Europe that implemented this disclosure requirement before 2016 (Audit Analytics, 2020b). However, prior to 2016, other jurisdictions in Europe (apart from France) had already imposed audit reforms that others are yet to follow. In the UK (FRC, 2013) and the Netherlands (NBA, 2014), for instance, audit firms are required to disclose materiality thresholds in their audit reports along with other relevant information. Standard setters in both the UK and the Netherlands issued standards that require auditors to disclose the audit materiality threshold used for financial statement audits (Christensen et al., 2020). Investors and analysts in other parts of the world are now calling for similar disclosures (Doxey et al., 2020). France is yet to heed to the calls for these materiality disclosures in audit reports.

Traditionally, French regulators have been highly restrictive in relation to NAS. According to the French Commercial Code, auditors can only perform audit and audit-related services for the firms they audit. The Code de Déontologie (French code of ethics) provides further detailed guidelines and poses strong restrictions regarding the services that cannot be provided by the auditor and its network. These include the following: bookkeeping; preparation of financial information; services that require the auditor to prepare components of the client's business which are subject to evaluation in the statutory audit; managerial roles; recruitment of key personnel; legal services; finance management; audit of asset transfers or mergers; implementation of internal control systems; actuarial and other valuation services; design and implementation of financial information systems; legal, financial, or tax consulting on financing decisions; outsourcing activities; corporate finance and financing activities; and representing the client before any jurisdiction or appearing as an expert. Given this restrictive approach, the bans on NAS introduced by the EU Audit Reform (2014) barely affected French audit firms. Only tax, legal, and employee-related services were added to the list of prohibited services. As a result, France relies on the EU regulation for NAS restrictions without any exception (EU Parliament Report, 2019). According to the General Regulation issued by the Autorité des Marchés Financiers (AMF), the French financial markets regulator, listed companies in France are mandated to separately disclose audit and non-audit fees. Audit fees need to be split in actual audit fees, and fees directly related to the audit.

Because France is the only European country to have a mandatory joint audit requirement, it is a European country with the majority of joint PIEs' audit, representing 86% of total for the EU-28 (European Commission, 2021). Because of the joint audit requirement, France is also characterised by a higher number (3,431) of statutory audits of PIEs (European Commission, 2017). Big Four companies collectively account for just 57% of the overall market share among the largest listed companies in France (Audit Analytics, 2020b). This is much lower than in other countries as Germany, Italy, and the UK. However, this difference is also likely to be due to France's joint audit system.

2.4.4 *Italy*

The audit oversight system in Italy consists of the Ministry of Economy and Finance (MEF) and the *Commissione Nazionale per le Società e la Borsa* (CONSOB) (Delegated Decree No. 30/2010). The MEF is responsible for approving and registering statutory auditors, endorsing the auditing standards and the code of ethics for statutory auditors of non-PIEs, establishing a quality assurance review system for audits of non-PIEs, and implementing disciplinary measures and possible sanctions for statutory auditors of non-PIEs.

CONSOB is a national independent authority responsible for regulating the Italian financial markets. It regularly conducts investigations with respect to potential infringements of insider dealing and market law manipulation (Consob, 2019). With specific reference to audit of PIEs, CONSOB is responsible for adopting auditing standards, overseeing the audit firms' organisation and activities, monitoring the audit firms' independence and technical competence, establishing a quality assurance review system for statutory audits, and investigating and disciplining statutory auditors for misconduct and breach of the rules and legal requirements.

The statutory audit by a professional external auditor was introduced in 1975 for listed companies (Presidential decree No. 136/1975). Such regulation was particularly advanced, as Italy was one of the first countries in the world to legislate a nine-year mandatory audit firm rotation (three-year mandate, renewable for two additional three-year terms; Corbella et al., 2015). Provisions about mandatory audit firm rotation were revised several times, especially in the mid-2000s, when audit partner rotation was also mandated (Legislative Decree 58/1998; Law 262/2005; Legislative Decree 303/2006). Since 2010 (Legislative Decree 39/2010), audit firm rotation has been compulsory every nine years, and is renewable after a three-year cooling-off period. Conversely, audit partner rotation is mandatory every seven years, with a three-year cooling-off period. All provisions on mandatory rotation remain unchanged after the introduction of the EU audit reform in 2016. Since the introduction of statutory audit, the legislator has always paid particular attention to the NAS, to preserve the auditor's independence. However, the initial limitation requirement was quite vague (Ianniello, 2011), and CONSOB tried to enforce higher controls on NAS, by attributing to the BSA the duty of supervising any NAS attribution undertaken by the board of directors (CONSOB, 1997). The risks of such a regulatory *vacuum* were later connected to some of Italy's biggest accounting scandals, such as Cirio and Parmalat. Specifically, after the Parmalat scandal, in 2005 the regulator intervened with a more stringent regulation of NAS (Law 262/2005) by identifying in detail the incompatible activities, following the example of the Sarbanes-Oxley Act (SOX) of 2002. Subsequently, Legislative Decree 39/2010 provided that the audit firm in charge cannot offer to its client the following services: involvement in management or decision-making processes; bookkeeping and preparing of financial statements; payroll services; internal audit engagements; and corporate finance and financing services. Following the implementation of the EU Audit Reform (2014), the list of prohibited NAS activities has been enlarged and covers a wide range of tax services, the design and implementation of internal control or financial information technology, and human resources services. Italy's reliance is on the EU regulation for NAS restrictions, without any exception (EU Parliament Report, 2019). Moreover, Italian listed companies are required to disclose the audit fees and the NAS activities and fees in their annual reports (Legislative Decree 39/2010).

The audit market in Italy consists of 1,578 statutory audits of PIEs (European Commission, 2017). In 2019, five firms audited the largest 100 Italian listed companies. The Big Four account for 98% of the audit market share, with the remaining 2% (2 companies) being audited by BDO, the only non-Big Four (Audit Analytics, 2020c). By looking at the Big Four portfolio, revenues collected from audit services provided to PIEs are seen to be equal to 18% of total revenue (Cameran and Santoli, 2018).

2.5 Summary

The audit market in Europe is varied. In terms of size, a total number of 25,275 PIEs' statutory audits were recorded in the 28 EU countries in 2018, decreasing from the 29,254 recorded in 2015, with most of these statutory audits being produced in Spain and France (European Commission, 2017, 2021). Joint PIEs' audits represent only 9% of overall PIEs' statutory audits, with only ten Member States reporting joint audits and France having the most (86% of the EU-28 total). The audit market in Europe is highly concentrated in the hands of the Big Four. They are on average responsible for 70% of all PIE statutory audits and have an oligopoly position in 13 Member States, including the UK, Germany, and Italy (European Commission, 2021). Among the Member States in which the Big Four have an aggregate market share below the EU average, France is the only large economy. The Big Four are even more dominant in terms of the revenues arising from PIEs' statutory audits, with a share of around 80% of the EU market.

In relation to the implementation status of the EU Audit Reform (2014), Germany, France, and the UK were early adopters, around June 2016, whereas Italy adopted it after June 2016 (EU Parliament Report, 2019). In terms of mandatory auditor rotation, Germany and the UK have opted for a mandatory firm rotation period of ten years with an extension of a further ten years available on engagements of PIEs (flexible implementation). France also has a ten-year mandatory firm rotation period that can be extend to further 14 years, if there is a joint audit, and to 6 years, if there is no joint audit. In Italy the period is up to nine years with no extension option (strict implementation). In relation to NAS regulations, in Italy and Germany reliance is mostly on the EU regulation for NAS restrictions (EU Parliament Report, 2019). France and the UK have in place additional regulations to discipline NAS next to the EU regulation, although the UK has gone further than France. Together with the Netherlands, it requires mandatory materiality threshold disclosures in audit reports. In other parts of Europe these remain voluntary materiality disclosures; however, this appears to be the domain of what is mainly PwC audit clients (Kend and Nguyen, 2022).

Only in Scandinavia could one find voluntary disclosure of audit materiality judgements, and this is exclusively by PwC in Finland. In other Scandinavian countries, such as Sweden, for instance, PwC mentions limited information about audit materiality in their audit reports; however, only in Finland did they specify the overall materiality benchmarks reported and how these thresholds are determined. The perpetual state of change that has vibrated through the auditing profession has crossed boundaries that vary in time and space. The differences observed in Europe are because of this perpetual state of change, occurring when audit is operationalised into practice.

Notes

1 Some European countries have extended this requirement. For example, listed companies in Italy are also required to use IAS/IFRS for preparing their separate financial statement.
2 For a detailed analysis of the differences between national accounting standards and IFRS in France, Germany, Italy, and the Netherlands, please see KPMG (2019, 2021) and PWC (2019).
3 In Germany, employees and shareholders are considered as salient stakeholders that can exert substantial influence on managerial decision-making. According to the current regulation, employees have a right to appoint their representatives on the supervisory board of large companies. They have the right to appoint one-third of the members of the supervisory board in companies with the number of employees between 500 and 2,000 and half in companies with more than 2,000 employees. The remaining members of the supervisory board are appointed by the general assembly of shareholders.
4 In Germany, thanks to a proxy voting system (called Depotstimmrecht), banks have the right to exercise the voting rights conferred to them by customers who do not want to exercise this right themselves (Baums et al., 1994).
5 The current regulation requires all PIEs and commercial companies that exceed at least two of the three following thresholds, (i) turnover of 8 EUR mil, total assets of 4 EUR mil, and (iii) 50 employees to appoint an auditor.

References

Aguilera, R. V., and Cuervo-Cazurra, A. (2004). Codes of good governance worldwide: what is the trigger? *Organization Studies*, 25(3): 415–443.

Aguilera, R. (2005). Corporate governance and employment relations: Spain in the context of Western Europe. *Corporate Governance and Labour Management: An International Comparison*, pp. 197–225, Working Papers 04-0101, University of Illinois at Urbana-Champaign, College of Business.

Audit Analytics (2020a). Who audits public companies – Germany. Available at: https://blog.auditanalytics.com/who-audits-public-companies-germany-2020/. Accessed on 05.02.22.

Audit Analytics (2020b). Who audits public companies – Germany. Available at: https://blog.auditanalytics.com/who-audits-public-companies-germany-2020/. Accessed on 05.02.22.

Audit Analytics (2020c). Who audits public companies – Italy. Available at: https://blog.auditanalytics.com/who-audits-public-companies-italy-2020/. Accessed 05.02.22.

Baums, T. (1992). Corporate governance in Germany: The role of the banks. *The American Journal of Comparative Law,* 40(2): 503–526.

Baums, T., Aoki, M., and Patrick, H. (Eds.) (1994)., *The Japanese main bank system: Its relevance for developing and transforming economies.* Oxford: Oxford University Press, pp. 409–449

Ben Ben-Nasr, H., Boubaker, S., and Rouatbi, W. (2015). Ownership structure, control contestability, and corporate debt maturity. *Journal of Corporate Finance,* 35: 265–285.

Bonacchi, M., Cipollini, F., and Zarowin, P. (2018). Parents' use of subsidiaries to "push down" earnings management: Evidence from Italy. *Contemporary Accounting Research,* 35(3): 1332–1362.

Burgstahler, D. C., Hail, L., and Leuz, C. (2006). The importance of reporting incentives: Earnings management in European private and public firms. *The Accounting Review*, 81(5): 983–1016.

Cameran, M., and Santoli, E. (Eds) (2018). Il mercato della revisione contabile in Italia al 31-12-2017. SDA Bocconi - Osservatorio di Revisione. Available at: http://osservatoriorevisione.sdabocconi.it/

Christensen, B., Eilifsen, A., Glover, S., and Messier Jr, W. (2020). The effect of audit materiality disclosures on investors' decision making. *Accounting, Organizations and Society,* in press, 87. https://doi.org/10.1016/j.aos.2020.101168.

Commissione Nazionale per le Società e la Borsa – Consob (1997). Comunicazione n. DAC/RM/97001574 del 20-02-1997. Raccomandazioni in material di controlli societari. Available at: http://www.consob.it/documents/46180/46181/97001574.pdf/dd50ace4-ac64-4aa2-9a9e-8990bb899cbf

Commissione Nazionale per le Società e la Borsa – Consob (2019). Testo Unico della Finanza. Available at: http://www.consob.it/documents/46180/46181/dlgs58_1998.pdf/e15d5dd6-7914-4e9f-959f-2f3b88400f88

Competition and Market Authority – CMA (2018). *Statutory audit services market study.* London: National Archives.

Coram, P.J., and Wang, L. (2020). The effect of disclosing key audit matters and accounting standard precision on the audit expectation gap., *International Journal of Auditing,* 25(2): 270–282.

Corbella, S., Florio, C., Gotti, G., and Mastrolia, S. A. (2015). Audit firm rotation, audit fees and audit quality: The experience of Italian public companies. *Journal of International Accounting, Auditing and Taxation,* 25: 46–66.

Dattin, C.F. (2017). Developments in France regarding the mandatory rotation of auditors: Do they enhance auditors' independence? *Accounting History,* 22(1): 44–66.

Davis, G. F., and Kim, S. (2015). Financialization of the economy. *Annual Review of Sociology*, 41(1): 203–221.

De Jong, H.W. (1989). The takeover market in Europe: Control structures and the performance of large companies compared. *Review of Industrial Organization,* 6: 1–18.

Doxey, M., Hatfield, R., Rippy, J., and Peel, K. (2020). Asymmetric investor materiality and the effects of disclosure. *Auditing: A Journal of Practice & Theory,* 39(2): 27–50.

ECGI (n.d.). Codes. Available at: https://ecgi.global/content/codes. Accessed 05.02.22.

Enriques, L., and Volpin, P. (2007). Corporate governance reforms in continental Europe. *Journal of Economic Perspectives*, 21(1): 117–140.

European Commission (2017). Report on monitoring developments in the EU market for providing statutory audit services to public-interest entities pursuant to Article 27 of Regulation (EU) 537/2014. Available at: https://eur-lex.europa.eu/legal-content/EN/TXT/PDF/?uri=CELEX:52017DC0464&from=EN

European Commission (2021). Report from the commission to the European Parliament, the council, the European Central Bank, and the European systemic risk board on developments in the EU market for statutory audit services to public-interest entities pursuant to article 27 of regulation (EU) no 537/2014. Available at: https://eur-lex.europa.eu/legal-content/EN/TXT/PDF/?uri=-CELEX:52021DC0029&rid=10. Accessed 05.02.22.

European Parliament (2019). EU Statutory Audit Reform Impact on costs, concentration and competition. Available at https://www.europarl.europa.eu/RegData/etudes/STUD/2019/631057/IPOL_STU(2019)631057_EN.pdf. Accessed 05.02.22.

European Union (EU) (2014a). Directive 2006/43/EC of the European Parliament and of the Council of 17 May 2006 on statutory audits of annual accounts and consolidated accounts. Available at: https://eur-lex.europa.eu/legal-content/EN/TXT/HTML/?uri=CELEX:32014L0056&from=EN. Accessed 15.03.19.

European Union (EU) (2014b). Regulation (EU) No 537/2014 of the European parliament and of the council of 16 April 2014 on specific requirements regarding statutory audit of public-interest entities and repealing Commission Decision 2005/909/EC. Available at: http://eur-lex.europa.eu/legal-content/EN/TXT/PDF/?uri=CELEX:32014R0537&from=EN. Accessed 15.03.19.

Ferrarini, G., Moloney, N., and Ungureanu, M. C. (2010). Executive remuneration in crisis: a critical assessment of reforms in Europe. *Journal of Corporate Law Studies,* 10(1): 73–118.

Financial Reporting Council – FRC (2012). The UK Stewardship Code, Financial Reporting Council, London. Available at https://www.frc.org.uk/investors/uk-stewardship-code

Financial Reporting Council (FRC). (2013). International Standard on Auditing (UK and Ireland) 700: The independent auditor's report on financial statements (revised June 2013). June. Available at: https://www.frc.org.uk/Our-Work/Publications/Audit-and-Assurance-Team/ISA-700-(UK-and-Ireland)-700-(Revised)-File.pdf.

Financial Reporting Council – FRC (2018). The UK Corporate Governance Code, Financial Reporting Council, London. Available at: https://www.frc.org.uk/getattachment/88bd8c45-50ea-4841-95b0-d2f4f48069a2/2018-UK-Corporate-Governance-Code-FINAL.pdf

Goergen, M., and Renneboog, L. (2001). Investment policy, internal financing and ownership concentration in the UK. *Journal of Corporate Finance,* 7(3): 257–284.

Goergen, M., Manjon, M.C., and Renneboog, L. (2008). Is the German system of corporate governance converging towards the Anglo-American model? *Journal of Management & Governance,* 12(1): 37–71.

Gray, S. J. (1988). Towards a theory of cultural influence on the development of accounting systems internationally. *ABACUS,* 24(1): 1–15.

Hackethal, A., Schmidt, R.H., and Tyrell, M. (2005). Banks and German Corporate Governance: On the way to a capital market-based system? *Corporate Governance: An International Review,* 13(3): 397–407.

Hohenfels, D., and Quick, R. (2020). Non-audit services and audit quality: Evidence from Germany. *Review of Managerial Science,* 14(5): 959–1007.

Ianniello, G. (2011). Indicatori sull'indipendenza (in apparenza) del revisore contabile: il caso della prestazione di servizi non di revisione. *Economia Aziendale Online,* 2(1): 45–56.

International Auditing and Assurance Standards Board (IAASB) (2013). "A framework for audit quality". Consultation Paper.

ISA (701) (International Auditing Assurance Standards Board) (2015). International Standard on Auditing (ISA) 701, Communicating Key Audit Matters in the Independent Auditor's Report. International Federation of Accountants New York.

Jensen, M. C., and Meckling, W. H. (1979). Rights and production functions: An application to labor-managed firms and codetermination. *Journal of Business,* 52(4): 469–506.

Keasey, K., Short, H., and Wright, M. (2005). The development of corporate governance codes in the UK. *Corporate Governance: Accountability, Enterprise and International Comparisons,* 21–45.

Keasey, K., Thompson, S., and Wright, M. (Eds.). (1997). *Corporate governance: Economic and financial issues.* Oxford: OUP.

Kend, M., and Nguyen, L. (2022). How audit materiality has been translated into existing audit spaces: Competing logics and different outcomes in Australia and New Zealand. *Critical Perspectives on Accounting,* (in press).

KPMG (2015). The new auditor's report: Greater transparency, more relevant. Available at: https://assets.kpmg.com/content/dam/kpmg/cn/pdf/en/2016/12/the-new-auditorreport.pdf. Accessed 20.06.21.

KPMG (2019). IFRS compared to French GAAP: An overview. Available at: https://assets.kpmg/content/dam/kpmg/fr/pdf/2019/09/fr-global-assurance-ifrs-compared-french-gaap-overview_sept19.pdf

KPMG (2021). IFRS compared to German GAAP and Dutch GAAP. Available at: https://hub.kpmg.de/hubfs/LandingPages-PDF/KPMG_IFRS%20vs%20HGB%20vs%20Dutch_sec_bf.pdf?utm_campaign=Handbook%20-%20IFRS%20compared%20to%20German%20GAAP%20and%20Dutch%20GAAP&utm_medium=email&_hsmi=118815845&_hsenc=p2ANqtz-8ZrH-cyNzKb8FECotpxtpO0r-8sws1AuebVsENVBopo9O0gls82_7jXMNMt0P-dcSWVHd9Tx6T3uo_sfZ5f_3z-MpuaRNg&utm_content=118815845&utm_source=hs_automation

La Porta, R., Lopez-de-Silanes, F., and Shleifer, A. (1999). Corporate ownership around the world. *The Journal of Finance,* 54(2): 471–517.

La Porta, R., Lopez-de-Silanes, F., Shleifer, A., and Vishny, R. W. (1998). Law and finance. *Journal of Political Economy,* 106(6): 1113–1155.

La Porta, R., Lopez-de-Silanes, F., Shleifer, A., and Vishny, R. W. (2000). Investor protection and corporate governance. *Journal of Financial Economics,* 58(1–2): 3–27.

Lorsch, J.W., and MacIver, E. (1989). *Pawns or potentates: The reality of America's corporate boards.* Boston, MA: Harvard Business School Press.

Mallin, C. (2016). *Corporate governance.* Oxford: Oxford university press.

Meek, G. K., and Thomas, W. B. (2004). A review of markets-based international accounting research. *Journal of International Accounting Research,* 3(1): 21–41.

Melis, A. (2000). Corporate governance in Italy. *Corporate Governance: An International Review,* 8(4): 347–355.

Melis, A., and Rombi, L. (2018). Are optimal contracting and managerial power competing or complementary views? Evidence from the compensation of statutory auditors in Italy. *Corporate Governance: An International Review,* 26(3): 197–218.

Melis, A., and Zattoni, A. (2017). A primer on corporate governance: Italy. New York: Business Expert Press.

Millet-Reyes, B., and Zhao, R. (2010). A comparison between one-tier and two-tier board structures in France. *Journal of International Financial Management & Accounting,* 21(3): 279–310.

Moerland, P.W. (1995). Alternative disciplinary mechanisms in different corporate systems. *Journal of Economic Behavior & Organization,* 26(1): 17–34.

Nederlandse Beroepsorganisatie van Accountants (NBA). (2014). *Standard 702N: Additions regarding the reporting on a complete set of general-purpose financial statements at a public interest entity.* Amsterdam: NBA.

Niyama J. (2010). *Contabilidade internacional.* 2nd ed. São Paulo: Atlas.

OECD (2012). *Board member nomination and election.* Paris: OECD Publishing. http://dx.doi.org/10.1787/9789264179356-en

OECD (2021). *OECD corporate governance factbook 2021.* Paris: OECD Publishing.

Peecher, M. E., Solomon, I., and Trotman, K. T. (2013). An accountability framework for financial statement auditors and related research questions. *Accounting, Organizations and Society,* 38(8): 596–620.

PWC (2019). Financial statements: Looking to the future. Available at: https://www.pwc.com/it/it/publications/assets/docs/oic-2019.pdf

Quick, R., Schenk, N., Schmidt, F., and Towara, T. (2018). The impact of corporate governance on auditor choice: Evidence from Germany. *Journal of Management and Governance,* 22: 251–283. Available at: https://link.springer.com/content/pdf/10.1007/s10997-017-9386-4.pdf

Ratzinger-Sakel, N.V., and Schönberger, M.W. (2015). Restricting non-audit services in Europe – The potential (lack of) impact of a blacklist and a fee cap on auditor independence and audit quality. *Accounting in Europe,* 12(1): 61–86.

Tilba, A., and McNulty, T. (2013). Engaged versus disengaged ownership: The case of pension funds in the UK. *Corporate Governance: An International Review,* 21(2): 165–182.

Weimer, J., and Pape, J. (1999). A taxonomy of systems of corporate governance. *Corporate Governance: An International Review,* 7(2): 152–166.

Zattoni, A. (1999). The structure of corporate groups: The Italian case. *Corporate Governance: An International Review*, 7(1): 38–48.

Zingales, L. (1994). The value of the voting right: A study of the Milan stock exchange experience. *The Review of Financial Studies,* 7(1): 125–148.

3 New audit reports

Improving informational content and value

3.1 Introduction

Over the past two decades, three factors have resulted in regulators around the world fundamentally changing the content of the external audit report (Vanstraelen et al., 2012; Mock et al., 2013; Bédard et al., 2016). First, following the 2007–2008 Global Financial Crisis (GFC) and previous high-profile corporate scandals, the public has lost some confidence in the global capital markets and increasingly questioned the credibility of external auditors (Minutti-Meza, 2021). Second, a wide array of knowledgeable users of financial reporting perceived a gap between the information they desire and the information provided in the external audit report (Minutti-Meza, 2021). This information gap is a component of a broader disparity between users' beliefs about the external auditor's responsibilities and the external auditor's procedures, objectives, and responsibilities (Minutti-Meza, 2021). Third, regulators and audit standard setters perceived a growing need to revisit the statutory audit report to make it more relevant than a pass/fail opinion indicating whether a company's financial statements comply with accounting standards (Minutti-Meza, 2021).

In Chapter 3 we present the impacts generated by the introduction of the extended audit report in two European countries, namely, the UK and Italy. Insights on the impacts of the extended audit report are still scant in the audit literature and this chapter provides initial evidence within the European setting. Having the chance to collect the perspectives of audit practitioners and other stakeholders via focus groups and interviews, we offer an overview of the perceived impacts of the extended audit report in two countries that have different approaches towards audit and regulation, thereby well representing the diversity that characterises the European setting.

3.2 Overview of the new extended audit reports

The EU (European Union) Audit Reform (2014) has strengthened the information requirement of the audit reports, especially with reference to public interest entities (PIEs), thereby extending the traditional audit report. The

DOI: 10.4324/9781003262596-3

EU was driven by the need to make the audit report more informative for investors by providing them with relevant information about the audited company, rather than a mere standardised opinion on the financial statements. Amid the mounting demand for more informative and relevant audit reports, auditing regulators around the world and not just the EU have considered enhancing the audit report (Minutti-Meza, 2021; Zeng et al., 2021).

The extended audit report was introduced by EU regulators with two aims. The first is to provide a real focus on the issues that were being addressed in the audit. There is a set of requirements for audit committees in relation to these issues. The second is to have the auditors stating more information about the audit itself. Whether this has led to more standardisation with other EU Member States is open to debate, but at the same time there is now more scope for auditors to explain their judgements. Both the UK and Italy have implemented the extended audit report, although at different points in time. This reform has affected the UK and Italian auditors differently, especially in their managerial and organisational practices and their relationships with the client's management and other stakeholders. This new generation of audit reports includes disclosures about significant matters in a company's financial reporting and its audit (Minutti-Meza, 2021). These disclosures are a landmark change in auditors' responsibility to provide information to shareholders (Minutti-Meza, 2021).

Recently, regulators worldwide have sought to improve transparency around the audit process by implementing significant changes to auditor reporting (Reid et al., 2015). The International Auditing and Assurance Standards Board (IAASB) implemented a new auditing standard (ISA 701) that became effective on 15 December 2016, which requires auditors to disclose key audit matters in their reports (IAASB, 2015). The new form audit reports include a section termed "key audit matters (KAMs)." The introduction of KAMs is considered one of the most significant changes to the audit reporting model in the past 90 years (Coram and Wang, 2020). The purpose of KAMs is to disclose financial reporting risks, thus enhancing the communication value of the external audit report to shareholders. KAMs are financial reporting matters that, in the external auditor's professional judgement, require significant auditor attention during the statutory audit engagement (ASA 701/ISA 701). KAMs are determined from the same pool of matters communicated to those charged with governance (ISA 701, para. 7) and they require external auditors to consider issues where there is a high risk of misstatement (or error), where there is significant management judgement involved, and where the effect of a transaction is considered significant. When disclosing KAMs, the standard requires the external auditor to explain why the matter is important, how it was addressed, and to reference any relevant financial statement disclosures (Nguyen and Kend, 2021). Some researchers and commentators believe that the new KAM audit reporting requirements are likely to increase auditors' accountability and professional scepticism, which should result in improved audit quality

(Peecher et al., 2013). Others suggest that the new KAM audit reporting requirements may impose additional pressure on auditors, and thus have an adverse effect on audit quality (KPMG, 2015). These mixed views ensure research is needed to explore the perceived impact of all these reforms on audit quality and how auditors' practices have changed in response to these audit reforms.

3.3 Impacts of extended audit reports

As a result of several UK reforms before the EU Audit Reform (2014), the UK had seen more pages appear in audit reports and there had been more careful consideration of the wording of those reports, which are no longer standardised. In the UK (FRC, 2013), for instance, audit firms disclose materiality thresholds in their audit reports along with other relevant information. Standard setters in both the UK and the Netherlands issued standards that require auditors to disclose the audit materiality threshold used for financial statement audits (Christensen et al., 2020). Investors and analysts in other parts of the world have subsequently been calling for similar disclosures (Doxey et al., 2020). For example, one CFA Institute survey reported that approximately four out of five financial analysts from around the world desire audit materiality disclosures (CFAI 2013, p. 80). Kend and Nguyen (2022a) report that in Scandinavia there is some voluntary disclosure of audit materiality judgements, and this is exclusively by PwC in Finland. In other Scandinavian countries such as Sweden, PwC mentions limited information about audit materiality in their audit reports; but only in Finland did they specify the overall materiality benchmarks in their reporting and how these thresholds are determined (Kend and Nguyen, 2022a). There is some voluntary disclosure and reporting of audit materiality information in both Australian and New Zealand audit reports (Kend and Basioudis, 2018). Australia is in a unique position (apart from Finland) where only one of the Big Four auditors, PwC, voluntarily discloses audit materiality thresholds. However, across the Tasman in New Zealand, three of the Big Four auditors voluntarily disclose audit materiality thresholds in audit reports (Kend and Nguyen, 2022a). In Australia there is reported resistance to audit materiality disclosures as per Kend and Nguyen (2022a), as stakeholder concerns shared with the researchers include that these voluntary audit materiality disclosures in audit reports would create confusion for investors and other potential users of audited financial statements and create risks for auditors such as management interference and litigation exposure.

There is an acknowledgement in the UK that the extended audit reports are now quite long. We can summarise the organisational impacts on the UK auditors due to the EU reforms very briefly, as many of the changes to UK audit reports had already been implemented before the 2016 EU reforms. Mainly, the concerns raised in the UK were that, due to increased regulatory scrutiny, auditors' risk management systems and internal quality controls within audit firms had to be improved, and that this was a distraction from the audit process and reporting side. However, in Italy the EU audit report reforms were much more profound in their impacts on organisational practices and audit processes.

In the UK, internally, firms are doing things more centrally, so that they can help their more senior auditors to deal with these reviews and constant scrutiny. In the UK the auditors have Audit Quality Reviews (AQRs) designed to ensure that documentation is complete and standardised, and over time these controls are becoming more automated. In the UK the interview respondents indicated that risk management systems have been recalibrated to produce complete documentation, but some concerns were noted. Indeed, some UK interview respondents underlined that there has been a need to improve the internal risk management system, but that this has distracted auditors from their main activity, which is to audit the financial statements and produce the audit report.

If we move our attention to Italy, Italian Big Four auditors agree that the extended audit report EU reform has introduced a significant change for the organisation and management of their audit activity after the EU reform was enforced in 2016. Like the UK, they have recognised how the length of the audit report has increased. From a 2-page report, auditors are now preparing a 6- to 12-page audit report. We can summarise the organisational impact on Italian auditors in terms of three main impacts: (1) the need to plan their auditing tasks; (2) the greater involvement of more senior or experienced auditors for quality controls throughout the auditing process; and (3) the incremental rise in the number of verifications required during the audit process. This indicates that Italian auditors were more affected by the extension of the audit report than the UK auditors.

First, auditors in Italy need to plan their activities, as the extended audit report requires anticipating phases of the audit process that "had formerly been" carried out in the final stages of the work. Indeed, before the EU reform, the reporting phase was reasonably simple, as the report was expected to be only two to three pages long and structured into four paragraphs. This specific issue was not raised by the UK interview participants. Before the EU reform, their time (Italian auditors) was mostly spent reviewing the financial statements, while the report preparation was less time-consuming, especially due to its standardisation and its briefness:

> *[...] back to the impact on organisational processes, there has certainly been a significant anticipation of many reporting related activities.*
>
> (Big Four auditor, Verona, 2018)

Second, facing the changes in the audit report, Italian Big Four auditors respond to the additional information required by involving a larger number of professional experts in the audit teams allocated to a specific PIE. This choice is not reported by the UK interview participants, who are not referring to any extensions to their audit teams. In Italy, the tendency is to have a so-called Engagement Quality Reviewer (EQR) reviewing the audit team's work. The EQR is usually an audit partner in charge of verifying the audit report and the KAMs identified by the audit team. Since the implementation of the extended audit report, a technical director also supports the EQR's review. The technical expert is called upon to exert control across all the audit reports prepared by the audit partner, thereby providing a sort of standardisation across these reports; the technical expert thus appoints someone highly experienced from the same firm to control and provide an objective judgement of the audit done. Especially with the introduction of the extended audit report, the Italian auditors recognise the key role of more experienced auditors to supervise the entire audit process for their PIE clients. Indeed, the experience of the audit partner is increasingly a discriminating factor in the choice of the auditor by the clients and their audit committee/Board of Statutory Auditors (BSA).

Third, auditors in Italy have increased the number of verifications that they perform during the entire auditing of the client, as these verifications are also to be shown in the report as evidence of the auditor's ability to detect frauds and irregularities. By contrast, such an impact is not mentioned by any of the UK interview participants. This has also called for a slight increase in the working hours of managers and senior auditors, who are now more involved in the process. The verifications mainly focus on checking correspondences between what is reported and what has been effectively done during the auditing process. Because the audit report now includes a non-standardised part that is focused on the specifics of the audited entity (KAMs), the auditors must verify consistency with the audit activity carried out and the key risks initially identified.

> *[...] drawing up a report is now a more complex and delicate activity. And it has required, at least for this first year of implementation, a greater involvement of both the Managing Partner and the Engagement Quality Reviewer (EQR) [...] but also of an internal reviewer responsible for verifying the correspondence between what is said and what is effectively done.*
>
> (Big Four auditor, Verona, 2018)

3.3.1 Impacts on auditor's relation with the client

In the UK, when we asked about the impacts on the auditors' relationship with clients, many of the interview participants indicated that the extended audit report has generally improved this relationship by better demonstrating: (1) the application of professional scepticism; and (2) the challenges they face with company management. As the auditors are required to say a bit more about the audit than in the past (mainly due to the reporting of KAMs), this has been perceived as an opportunity to provide more information and disclosure about the audit process to the outside world. As a result, these reforms are perceived to have given auditors not only some responsibilities to talk about the issues surrounding the audit in the report but also the opportunity to give financial statement users some sense of what the audit looks like in terms of scope.

> *I think a well-written extended audit report which the auditor of course puts in quite a lot of thought into demonstrating how it is applied with scepticism, then touch on points, which give the sense of the challenges it's had with management and the big granularity which looked into some of the estimates and judgments.*
>
> (Non-Big Four auditor, London, 2018)

In the UK some of the interview respondents indicated that internal quality control processes had changed, driven by complete documentation demand and the need to observe professional scepticism with their clients in practice. Indeed, the admission that the management of internal quality control systems is a time-consuming activity, and the allegation that it is not always easy for the regulator during its inspection work to detect the auditor's practice of professional scepticism, both indicate that the logic or thinking of the UK regulator diverts from that of the UK auditors. The UK auditors appear to struggle to follow a logic that is not totally aligned with their need to focus on audit tasks and that doubts their professional scepticism in audit practice with clients. Most interview participants in the UK indicated that the audit report has somewhat changed compared to the one usually drawn up for clients before the implementation of the EU Audit Regulation (2014), but that the opportunity to better demonstrate how they apply professional scepticism to both clients and the public has helped increase information on the auditors' work, judgements, and communications with client management.

Auditors in Italy indicated that the extended audit report has affected their relationships with the clients also, but to a much greater degree than we observed in the UK. Two of the main impacts highlighted by the focus groups are: (1) the need to share more information with the client; and (2) the extension of the number of executives to which the auditors now communicate. The auditors in Italy indicated that, due to the innovations introduced by the extended audit report, they need to adequately inform their clients about the changes. Especially in the first year of the reform implementation, auditors stated that, on top of auditing activities, they were required to inform and educate their clients about the content of the EU reform. They underlined their clients' lack of knowledge about the changes due to the EU reform. To prevent any later problems or misunderstanding in the report preparation, they had to arrange preparation meetings to properly instruct their clients' top management and audit committees. After this initial informative phase, the communication and information sharing were indicated as ongoing throughout the auditing process, especially with the audit committee/BSA. One crucial aspect underlined by Italian auditors refers to the number of extra hours worked to draft the extended audit report for audit clients:

> *Working hours have slightly increased since there have been some reviews in this activity usually carried out by the partner manager of the audit team. Unfortunately, it is hard to receive recognition for these extra hours: we tried to count them in an anticipatory way as per the proposals made during that year, but it is more difficult for ongoing activities [...]*
>
> (Big Four auditor, Verona, 2018)

In Italy, before the introduction of the extended audit report, the main person of reference for the auditors during their auditing activities was the Chief Financial Officer (CFO). The CFO has a pivotal role for the auditors as the subject in charge of the financial statement preparation and with extensive knowledge of the company's accounts. However, with the changes from the EU reform, auditors in Italy reportedly now deal with topics that can fall outside the CFO's administrative scope, thereby having to refer directly to the top management. The additional topics regarding the company's methods to estimate and prevent risks, which are now part of the extended audit report, require that the auditors have direct contact and communication with the Chief Executive Officer (CEO) or other representatives of the top management. This is indicated as a significant change, as auditors had previously referred only to the CFO:

> *The CFO has always been our main reference point, while we never had direct relationship with the CEO. In this case instead we have almost been compelled to involve the top management [...]*
>
> (Big Four auditor, Milan, 2018)

3.3.2 Impacts on auditor's relation with the capital market and other stakeholders

The findings from the UK indicate that the extended audit reports are an improvement over the old form audit reports, mainly because of: (1) increased accessibility to information on the auditors' work; and (2) materiality threshold disclosures. The extended audit reports have given external auditors a licence to think out of the box and be more creative, and to have more freedom to express how they reached their audit judgements:

> *I know a lot of people who [...] tell me that it [the extended audit report] has focused their minds. It has given them an element of*

creativity that they didn't have before to say what they really think. We have put power in the hands of audit partners and senior managers to come up with and describe things that they say in an audit report.

(Big Four auditor, London, 2018)

There is a perception among the UK interview participants that more investors are reading the audit report compared to three to four years back, as they are provided with more information:

[...] the extended audit report definitely gives investors something to grab onto. I think more investors [...] are reading them than three or four years ago.

(Regulator, London, 2018)

Although it is difficult to say if investors value the extended audit reports for their investment decision-making, as trading updates are usually preferred to the audit report by investors; investors indicated some appreciation to the extent of non-financial information that is now presented in the extended audit reports:

I think it [the report] has been improved. I've been looking quite increasingly, and I'm really astonished by some of more information there is [...] and I also didn't quite believe the extent of non-financial information presented.

(Investor, London, 2018)

Beyond the investors, there is an expectation that financial analysts are reading and appreciating the extended audit report:

[...] As a matter of record the analysts can and should be reading it and the analysts understanding of what's going on [...].

(Regulator, London, 2018)

Consideration could be given to the ordering of the information that goes into the extended audit reports, although this was not raised by many UK interview participants. In addition, in the UK materiality thresholds are disclosed (and have been since around 2013), whereas in Italy this has not been the case. Academic research has sought to explore how audit materiality is given meaning and how it is operationalised in practice (Edgley, 2014). Although the audit report describes the concept of material misstatements, the impact of audit materiality on the scope and conduct of the audit largely remains publicly unavailable, thus contributing to the lack of empirical research on this topic (Houghton et al., 2011; Kend and Nguyen, 2022a). Critical studies have highlighted a lack of transparency in the concept of audit materiality (Kend and Nguyen, 2022a). Research indicates the term is not well specified or applied consistently (Brennan and Gray, 2005; Bolt and Tregidga, 2022; Kend and Nguyen, 2022a). The institutionalisation of the concept in auditing standards has resulted in the view that external auditors are being materialistic, calculating consequences rather than considering their duties (Shaub, 2005). Thus, audit materiality remains an enigmatic problem (Edgley, 2014; Kend and Nguyen, 2022a).

In the UK, materiality disclosures were generally seen in a positive light, as a UK reform that genuinely assists in narrowing the audit expectations gap. Some participants indicated that – out of all the additional disclosures in audit reports – materiality thresholds and the related information were the single most important reform:

> *If anything, that we've done over the last 10, 20, 30 years to help address the audit expectation gap, I think this [materiality disclosures] has done more for that than anything else has done up until this point, but it is more than just putting the numbers on the audit report.*
>
> (Big Four auditor, London, 2018)

This statement above and some other sentiments or views shared with us during the focus groups send a strong message on the importance of the materiality threshold disclosure. Reference was made to investors and how they might use materiality information, whether it is merely for them to be informed or to be acted on using the disclosures to assist with investment decisions. Although representing more work for auditors in the UK, the disclosure of materiality thresholds has been an especially welcomed reform by both audit committees and investors. The accessibility of knowing the materiality judgements, the transparency of the disclosures, and the subsequent user ability to understand what is going on may help to meet those user needs and expectations to some extent. Kend and Nguyen (2022a) report that in New Zealand any voluntary disclosure of audit materiality information helped to direct investors' attention to key areas of audit focus and gave them more insights into risk. Kend and Nguyen (2022a) reported on observations of improved quality in the communications between the audit committee and the external auditor due to the materiality disclosures in New Zealand.

On the downside, there has been a concern raised, albeit by only a few UK participants, that unsophisticated investors struggle to understand the concept of materiality. Prior research had conveyed similar concerns in other jurisdictions, like Australia (Houghton et al., 2011; Kend and Nguyen, 2022a). The rationale invoked is that, unless the whole concept of materiality was explained very well, providing only the audit materiality threshold and some other limited details may create uncertainty and the potential for undesirable misunderstandings (Houghton et al., 2011; Kend and Nguyen, 2022a). Investors interviewed in the Kend and Nguyen (2022a) study did not support the claims made by Australian external auditors, instead indicating that, in some circumstances, audit materiality disclosures would be helpful for some, suggesting that it should be up to investors to make their own judgements. There has, however, been agreement that sophisticated investors and some users of audited financial statements have a better capacity to understand the concept of materiality than retail investors (Houghton et al., 2011; Kend and Nguyen, 2022a). In the Houghton et al. (2011) study, there were concerns as to whether the actual level of audit materiality should be disclosed, with some of their interviewees feeling that it might be detrimental or dangerous. If company directors know the audit materiality threshold, there is the risk that they might attempt to step into the auditor's shoes and make materiality judgements or try to pressure auditors to adjust their audit materiality judgements (Houghton et al., 2011; Kend and Nguyen, 2022a).

A similar perception about investors' appreciation can be gathered from Italian participants; however, an opposite opinion arises regarding financial analysts. In Italy, auditors indicated that the extended audit report has also impacted their relationships with the market and other stakeholders. They identify two opposite reactions from the capital market: (1) more awareness of the investors about the auditor's job; and (2) analysts' silence about the new report.

First, Italian auditors show a general satisfaction regarding the extended audit report and how it has positively affected the capital market. Although auditors feared that, in view of the new audit report, the augmented disclosure would have exposed them to higher risks of being dismissed by clients or of lawsuits, they now recognise that the investors have appreciated the new form audit reports. While previously, the audit report's primary readers went straight to the audit report's conclusions, the whole of this extended audit report has gained their attention for the first time, and they are reportedly reading the entire audit report with more attention:

> *We [the auditors] always carry out the audit activity in the same way but we have changed the way we report it. [...] this is positive because, even if the extended audit report requires us to make a greater effort, it allows us to better communicate with third parties.*
>
> (Big Four auditor, Verona, 2018)

Appreciation on the higher transparency of the new audit report is confirmed by the Italian regulators who indicated:

> *Last year we analysed a sample of audit reports and noticed a bit of standardization across audit reports, with reference to KAMs. Clearly, all audit firms defined some guidelines that audit partners followed. Under certain points of view, this is also positive because using different terminology for delivering the same message would make it difficult to set the problem.*
>
> (Regulator, Rome, 2019)

Therefore, more attention is paid to the auditor's activity; and thus there are doubts expressed by some participants in Italy about the risks of misunderstanding, when the readers of the extended audit reports are not technically prepared. These doubts were expressed by some participants discussing the nature of the extended audit report:

> *[as a] technical tool that implies technical knowledge and culture not yet widespread in the Italian financial market.*
>
> (BSA member, Verona, 2019)

> *However, the main risk related to the fact of writing more things is that such things can be interpreted in several different ways depending on the reader.*
>
> (Big Four auditor, Verona, 2018)

In this respect, the extension of the disclosure about the audit activity may expose the auditors to responsibilities that are "*a bottomless pit*" (BSA member, Verona 2019). As a result, members of the audit committee/BSA call for more information and education around the audit activity to reduce the audit expectations gap. According to the participants, this is primarily important to:

> *Educate the market on what is and what is not the audit activity to avoid that the auditors are blamed for being responsible for any misstatement in the financial statements.*
>
> (BSA member, Verona, 2019)

Participants in Italy also feel the risk that, in case the auditor is sued because of the contents of the extended audit report and related activities, judges might misinterpret the issues because they lack adequate accounting and auditing competences, although judges could at any time seek expert explanations to inform their judgements.

As opposed to the UK perceptions, auditors in Italy indicated that, after the first year since the EU reform, financial analysts did not show any appreciation or concern about the content of the extended audit reports. Italian auditors seemed quite surprised about the lack of interest from the financial analysts, especially when compared to the UK. For instance, in the case of Citibank in the UK, the financial analysts issued a report stating that they found that the disclosure of auditors' work, as per the extended audit report, was useful information. However, among auditors in Italy, there is hope that the financial analysts' appreciation for the extended audit report will be just a matter of time and that they will convey more interest when the extended audit reports are issued in their second year of implementation.

> *I continue to think that, in Italy, it is too early, especially considering the average administrative culture. It is too early to bring this kind of*

documents to the attention of a wider audience, since, for example, the "significant risk" has a specific meaning for professional auditors, but not for those who do not have the necessary technical expertise in this sector.

(Big Four auditor, Verona, 2018)

3.4 Summary

With the extended audit reports has come a sense of improved accessibility to information about the auditors' work and their audit judgements. We noted standard setters in the UK issued standards between 2013 and 2014 that require auditors to disclose the audit materiality threshold. However, around that time both the IAASB and the Public Company Accounting Oversight Board (PCAOB) in the US decided to not require audit materiality disclosures (Christensen et al., 2020). The IAASB leaves audit materiality disclosures to the discretion of the auditors. In the US, the PCAOB does not discuss audit materiality disclosures by auditors in its standards.

In the UK, the materiality threshold disclosures are important to help in narrowing the audit expectations gap. However, in Italy there is a fear that this improved accessibility of information about the audit work will expose auditors to more risks of litigation. Kend and Nguyen (2022a) used an institutional logics perspective to better understand the fear auditors have related to being exposed to litigation risks due to materiality disclosures in audit reports. Within their theoretical framing is a legalistic logic reflecting a duty of care that external auditors have to shareholders as a group. Breaching this duty of care may result in litigation against the external auditors. To reduce litigation risk, external auditors will avoid reporting additional audit disclosures that are not mandated. In other words, they found that external auditors will protect their professional judgement from legal problems, by not voluntarily disclosing audit materiality thresholds. Further, Kend and Nguyen (2022a) apply the legalistic logic rationale suggesting it is extended to not only protecting shareholders but also protecting auditors themselves from breaching any duty of care to shareholders as a group. They observe a litigation-constrained, legalistic logic, where the resistance to change in practice or ideas is driven by the rationale to avoid potential litigation.

In Italy more so, some participants [all auditors] indicated that the extended audit report has affected their relationships with their clients and has led to significant changes in their organisational practices and in the management of their audit practices, whereas in the UK, the EU reform has not led to significant changes. Whereas in Italy the focus is on better communication with clients regarding these EU changes, the UK fears that constant regulatory scrutiny has perhaps been distracting for auditors, thus focusing them more on the demands for complete documentation rather than on the audit reporting for clients. In the UK as the Financial Reporting Council (FRC) had indicated implementation issues with the KAM reforms

(FRC, 2015), there were concerns expressed over the costs of the reforms' implementation, something that auditors highlighted in our study also. Meeting what clients now expect and balancing those expectations with fee constraints remains a challenge for all audit practitioners (Nguyen and Kend, 2021).

Since the implementation of the KAM reporting requirements, the environment in which audit judgements are made has changed substantially during the Coronavirus disease of 2019 (COVID-19) pandemic, and likely post-pandemic (Humphreys and Trotman, 2022). Research is needed on how COVID-19-related changes in the environment faced by auditors do affect external audit reports. At this stage, there is little academic research that has investigated how external auditors have responded to the COVID-19 pandemic and the associated audit risks that this crisis has created for their audit clients (Kend and Nguyen, 2022b). We know little about how changes in the COVID-19 environment affect audit tasks completed by external auditors (including judgements on what to include in external audit reports, particularly when disclosing the key audit risks). Albitar et al. (2020) suggest that the effects of the COVID-19 pandemic will be the toughest challenge for external auditors and their clients since the 2007–2008 GFC. Although beyond the scope of this present research, the authors acknowledge that in the future more consideration needs to be given to how the COVID-19 pandemic impacted audit tasks (i.e., specifically audit procedures), which have direct effects on key audit judgements and disclosures made in external audit reports related to audit risks.

Finally, policymakers in the EU should be interested in observing how auditors have responded when reporting on audit risk matters during a period of crisis. In Australia, for instance, the AUASB report (2020) proposed the following research question for the future: Has/will the impact of COVID-19 affect the reporting of KAMs? The AUASB (2020) states, "it will be interesting to examine the KAMs which reference COVID-19 in more detail to determine whether they have significantly changed from the previous year or simply carried over" (pp. 27–28). In the Australian study, Kend and Nguyen (2022b) provided some answers to this question by reporting on the number of audit procedures that referenced the COVID-19 pandemic within the KAMs section of audit reports in 2020. However, a similar study covering the EU would be a good and necessary contribution. Minutti-Meza (2021) claimed that expanded reports offer a promise that is yet to be fulfilled. For academics, Minutti-Meza (2021) emphasised exciting opportunities for future research on this topic – where there is still a need for definitive answers. For regulators and external auditors, Minutti-Meza (2021) underscored those existing requirements can simply be a first step towards enhanced auditor reporting that truly helps users to infer variation in financial reporting and audit quality (or significant risks).

References

Albitar, K., Gerged, A., Kikhia, H., and Hussainey, K. (2020). Auditing in times of social distancing: The effect of COVID-19 on auditing quality. *International Journal of Accounting & Information Management,* 29(1): 169–178. https://doi.org/10.1108/IJAIM-08-2020-0128

AUASB (2020). COVID-19 snapshot of auditor reporting in Australia. AUASB Research Report No. 5.

Bédard, J., Coram, P., Espahbodi, R., and Mock, T.J. (2016). Does recent academic research support changes to audit reporting standards? *Accounting Horizons,* 30(2): 255–275.

Bolt, R., and Tregidga, H. (2022). "Materiality is …": Sensemaking and sensegiving through storytelling. *Accounting, Auditing & Accountability Journal.* https://doi.org/10.1108/AAAJ-06-2021-5314

Brennan, N., and Gray S. (2005). The impact of materiality: accounting's best kept secret. *Asian Academy of Management Journal of Accounting and Finance,* 1: 1–31. Retrieved April 14, 2022, from http://web.usm.my/journal/aamjaf/vol1/1-1.pdf

CFA Institute (CFAI). (2013). *Financial reporting disclosures: Investor perspectives on transparency, trust, and volume.* New York, NY: CFA Institute.

Christensen, B., Eilifsen, A., Glover, S., and Messier Jr, W. (2020). The effect of audit materiality disclosures on investors' decision making. *Accounting, Organizations and Society,* 87(1). https://doi.org/10.1016/j.aos.2020.101168

Coram, P.J., and Wang L. (2020). The effect of disclosing key audit matters and accounting standard precision on the audit expectation gap. *International Journal of Auditing,* 25(2): 270–282. https://doi-org.ezproxy.lib.rmit.edu.au/10.1111/ijau.12203

Doxey, M., Hatfield, R., Rippy, J., and Peel, K. (2020). Asymmetric investor materiality and the effects of disclosure. *Auditing: A Journal of Practice & Theory,* 39(2): 27–50. https://doi.org/10.2308/ajpt-18-032

Edgley, C. (2014). A genealogy of accounting materiality. *Critical Perspectives on Accounting,* 25: 255–271. https://doi.org/10.1016/j.cpa.2013.06.001

Financial Reporting Council (FRC). (2013). International Standard on Auditing (UK and Ireland) 700: The independent auditor's report on financial statements (revised June 2013). Available at: https://www.frc.org.uk/Our-Work/Publications/Audit-and-Assurance-Team/ISA-700-(UK-and-Ireland)-700-(Revised)-File.pdf.

Financial Reporting Council (FRC). (2015). Financial reporting council—Transparency Reporting by Auditors of Public Interest Entities Review of Mandatory Reports [Online]. Accessed 20.12.2021.

Houghton, K. A., Jubb, C., and Kend, M. (2011). Materiality in the context of audit: The real expectations gap. *Managerial Auditing Journal,* 26(6): 482–500.

Humphreys, K., and Trotman, K. (2022). Judgment and decision-making research on CSR reporting in the COVID-19 pandemic environment. *Accounting and Finance,* 62(1): 739–765. https://doi.org/10.1111/acfi.12805

ISA (701) (International Auditing Assurance Standards Board) (IAASB) (2015). International Standard on Auditing (ISA) 701, Communicating Key Audit Matters in the Independent Auditor's Report. New York: International Federation of Accountants.

Kend, M., and Basioudis, I. (2018). Reforms to the market for audit and assurance services in the period after the Global Financial Crisis: Evidence from the UK. *Australian Accounting Review,* 28(4): 589–597. https://doi.org/10.1111/auar.12211

Kend, M., and Nguyen, L. (2022a). Translating audit materiality in disclosure: Competing logics and different outcomes in Australia and New Zealand. *Critical Perspectives on Accounting*, in press. https://doi.org/10.1016/j.cpa.2022.102502

Kend, M., and Nguyen, L. (2022b). Key audit risks and audit procedures during the initial year of the COVID-19 pandemic: An analysis of audit reports 2019–2020. *Managerial Auditing Journal,* 37(7): 798–818. https://doi.org/10.1108/MAJ-07-2021-3225

KPMG (2015). Transparency Report 2014. Available at: https://assets.kpmg.com/content/dam/kpmg/pdf/2016/01/transparency-report-2015.pdf

Minutti-Meza, M. (2021). The art of conversation: The expanded audit report. *Accounting and Business Research,* 51(5): 548–581. https://doi.org/10.1080/00014788.2021.1932264

Mock, T. J., Bédard, J., Coram, P. J., Davis, S. M., Espahbodi, R., and Warne, R. (2013). The audit reporting model: Current research synthesis and implications. *Auditing: A Journal of Practice and Theory*, 32(spl): 323–351.

Nguyen, L., and Kend, M. (2021). The perceived impact of the KAM reforms on audit reports, audit quality and auditor work practices: Stakeholders' perspectives. *Managerial Auditing Journal,* 36(3): 437–462. https://doi.org/10.1108/MAJ-10-2019-2445

Peecher, M.E., Solomon, I., and Trotman, K.T. (2013). An accountability framework for financial statement auditors and related research questions. *Accounting, Organizations and Society,* 38(8): 596–620.

Reid, L.C., Carcello, J.V., Li, C., and Neal, T.L. (2015). Impact of auditor and audit committee report changes on audit quality and costs: Evidence from the United Kingdom. Available at SSRN.

Shaub, M. (2005). Materialism and materiality. *International Journal of Accounting, Auditing and Performance Evaluation,* 2(5): 347–355. Retrieved April 15, 2022, from https://www.researchgate.net/profile/Michael-Shaub/publication/5171489_Materialism_and_materiality/links/02e7e53907a50630ea000000/Materialism-and-materiality.pdf

Vanstraelen, A., Schelleman, C., Meuwissen, R., and Hofmann, I. (2012). The audit reporting debate: Seemingly intractable problems and feasible solutions. *European Accounting Review*, 21(2): 193–215.

Zeng, Y., Zhang, J., Zhang, J., and Zhang, M. (2021). Key audit matters reports in China: Their descriptions and implications of audit quality. *Accounting Horizons,* 35(2): 167–192. https://doi.org/10.2308/HORIZONS-19-189

4 Mandatory audit firm rotation (MAFR)

Perceived benefits and costs

4.1 Introduction

In Chapter 4 we present the impacts of the EU (European Union) Audit Reform (2014) on mandatory audit firm rotation (MAFR). The EU Audit Reform (2014) has addressed auditor independence concerns by introducing (among other provisions) mandatory rotation at both the audit firm and the audit partner levels. Audit committees of public interest entities (PIEs) are now required to rotate auditors periodically, though the period may vary across Member States. The general rule is that the audit firms must be rotated at least every ten years. However, Member States may choose to reduce this period to a shorter period or may also permit PIEs to continue with the incumbent auditor for a maximum of 20 years if a transparent tender procedure has taken place, or for a maximum of 24 years if there have been joint audits.

It is important to acknowledge that all these options depend on the specific domestic legislation. In the UK after the Competition & Market Authority (CMA) review, from 2012 there was already some firm rotation to allay market competition concerns, although this was not mandatory (CMA, 2018). Following the 2014 EU Audit Reform and more in detail starting from 2016, the UK provides for an audit firm tenure of minimum three and maximum ten years for all PIEs. A cooling-off period of four years must be respected before the previous audit firm can be appointed again. These provisions have complemented the ones on audit partner rotation that was required even before the EU Audit Reform (2014) and takes place every five years with a cooling-off period of three years.

In Italy, MAFR was introduced early on, in 1975. A period of maximum nine years was established, as follows: initial three-year mandate, renewable for two additional three-year terms. Further mandatory rotation provisions were also introduced and repeatedly revised from the mid to late 2000s (Corbella et al., 2015). As a result, since 2010 in Italy, audit firm rotation is mandatory every nine years, with a cooling-off period of three years, while partner rotation is compulsory every seven years with a three-year cooling-off period. Such provisions were already fully compliant with the EU Audit Regulation (2014); thus the latter did not bring any significant change.

DOI: 10.4324/9781003262596-4

Over time, MAFR has represented a recurring matter of debate by auditing regulators around the world. For instance, in the US, the Sarbanes-Oxley Act (SOX) 2002 provided for audit partner rotation on an audit engagement of a public company every five years but did not require audit firm rotation. Likewise, in Australia, the CLERP (Corporate Law Economic Reform Program Proposals for Reform) 9 reforms introduced partner rotation very five years. In 2003, after having conducted a study on the potential effects of MAFR in the US, the General Accounting Office (GAO) concluded that it "*may not be the most efficient way to strengthen auditor independence and improve audit quality considering the additional financial costs and the loss of institutional knowledge of the company's previous audit firm of record*" (p. 1). The GAO thus suggested a "wait and see" attitude until the other reforms introduced by SOX were effective for several years. In 2011, the Public Company Accounting Oversight Board (PCAOB) issued a Concept Release where it considered MAFR to improve auditor independence, objectivity, and professional scepticism, but it faced strong opposition. Finally, in 2013, the Financial Services Committee of the US House of Representatives prohibited the PCAOB from requiring public companies to use specific audit firms and/or change audit firms on a rotating basis.

Interestingly, in the same year 2013, the European Parliament's Legal Affairs Committee approved a draft law that went in the opposite direction, introducing MAFR for all PIEs in the EU. This draft law brought in the provisions described above, which were a matter of discussion during our focus groups and interviewees. Although the Italian auditing regulation was already in line with the 2014 EU Audit Reform requirements, we gathered comments from Italian auditors on this aspect as well.

4.2 An overview of prior literature on MAFR

The benefits and costs of auditor rotation have long been discussed in the auditing literature both at a conceptual and at an empirical level. The main points of contention related to MAFR are those of auditor independence, audit quality, audit fees, and audit market concentration. Conceptually, auditor rotation is expected to be beneficial for an auditor's independence, as it avoids a tight and long-standing relationship between auditor and client firm. It is thus expected to be beneficial to audit quality, also because it brings a "fresh look" to the client's accounts. In such sense, audit firm rotation might solve some of the regulators' main concerns as regards audit quality. However, a loss of knowledge of the client's business dynamics is also recognised at the beginning of every new mandate, higher risk of audit failure in the first year(s) of engagement in a new client firm. Similarly, the possible effects of MAFR on audit fees and audit market competition are controversial. The new auditor is expected to bear set-up costs to understand the client's business model and organisational structure. At the same time, however, rotations might be used for negotiating lower average costs per hour of audit work, to the detriment of audit firms' profitability. In terms of market competition, it is argued that the MAFR restricts audit firm choice and forces client companies to select audit firms which do not have the same industry expertise as their current auditors. Another major issue discussed is the possible effect of MAFR on Big Four and non-Big Four companies: on the one hand, mandatory rotation is likely to grant to smaller audit firms the opportunity to grow; on the other hand, it is equally likely that it will lead to higher market concentration if large corporations continue to choose the Big Four when switching their audit firm (Ewelt-Knauer et al., 2013).

In their literature review on stakeholders' perceptions around MAFR, Ewelt-Knauer et al. (2013) found that extant evidence on the impacts of MAFR on audit quality and auditor independence is inconclusive and calls for further research on the issue. Throughout Europe, evidence provided by qualitative research based on surveys and interviews is still inconclusive. The results of an extensive survey submitted to UK practising accountants, auditors, and accounting academics after the Global Financial Crisis (GFC) indicate MAFR is a critical factor for enhancing statutory auditors (Aziz and Omoteso, 2014). In Germany, supervisory board members and management underline that MAFR is not expected to increase the benefits of audits: indeed, while it is expected to increase auditor independence and professional scepticism, it will bring a loss of client-specific expertise and knowledge (Ruhnke and Schmidt, 2014). In their turn, Austrian professional investment consultants from credit institutions do not perceive the MAFR beneficial to auditor independence and audit quality (Aschauer and Quick, 2018). Conversely, the members of the Institute of Certified Public Accountants of Greece agree that MAFR will determine an increase of auditor independence and of the resistance to the management of audited firms, but also of the overall costs of the audit process (Polychronidou et al., 2020).

Archival research has mainly investigated contexts where rotation was voluntary, with findings that tend to suggest MAFR is not worth it. In the US, Myers et al. (2003) found that longer tenure is associated with both income-increasing and income-decreasing accruals, thus resulting in higher audit quality. In Australia, Jackson et al. (2008) provided evidence that the propensity to issue a going concern opinion increases with audit tenure, while the level of discretionary expenses is not affected by audit tenure. In Spain, Garcia-Blandon et al. (2017) failed to collect empirical evidence on reduced audit quality when audit firm tenure is longer than 10 years and even when it is longer than 20 years, the second threshold established by EU Regulation (2014). Referring to a long timeframe just preceding the EU Audit Reform (2014), Garcia-Blandon et al. (2020) concluded that S&P Europe companies whose accounts are being audited by the same audit firm for over ten years do not show lower audit quality than the others. In terms of perceptions, however, Hohenfels (2016) revealed that German investors perceive the highest audit quality when the auditor tenure is around eight–nine years, while they perceive lower earnings quality in the early and later years of a mandate.

A notable exception as regards empirical archival research is the Italian setting, where MAFR rule was effective since 1975. Evidence there collected on the association between audit firm rotation and audit quality is mixed. Cameran et al. (2015) found no statistically significant association between MAFR and audit quality in public companies audited by Big Four audit firms. However, by examining public companies audited by both Big Four and non-Big Four over a 14-year time horizon, Corbella et al. (2015) found that audit quality improves following MAFR for those companies audited by a non-Big Four audit firm and that the improvement persists in the three years after the audit firm change. They also demonstrated that audit fees do not increase following MAFR yet remaining unchanged for companies audited by a non-Big Four and being lower for companies audited by a Big Four.

A small number of accounting studies have focused on the audit tendering process so far. A Dutch study by Taminiau and Heusinkveld (2017) focused on the audit tendering aspect of the MAFR requirement. Overall, they describe the tendering process as a dynamic process in which client expectations about the auditor's role evolve over time and that the auditors' actions are not only determined by the formal tendering procedures but also influenced by their level of agency. Moreover, Allam et al. (2017) specifically reviewed stakeholders' views in the UK on audit tendering. By conducting a content analysis of the comment letters sent to the Financial Reporting Council (FRC) in response to the consultation document on the 2012 revisions to the UK Corporate Governance Code, their study found conflicts of interest among some stakeholder groups such as audit firms and companies on one side and institutional investors on the other, and further evidence of conflicts of interest between Big Four and non-Big Four audit firms on audit tendering.

4.3 Impacts of MAFR

In what follows, we observe differential impacts from insights collected from both the UK and Italian auditors on the introduction of MAFR in the EU, partially due to their different implementation of the new regulations. In summary, especially in the UK, impacts were mainly positive, although some negative effects were indicated, whereas in Italy the impacts were minimal. While, for the UK, MAFR constitutes a significant change in audit practice, Italy has been dealing with such a norm, as well as mandatory partner rotation, for quite a while. Indeed, as mentioned earlier in this report, from 1975, Italy has adopted the MAFR of a nine-year period – and later a mandatory partner rotation of seven years. As a result, it is not surprising that, in Italy, auditors indicate that the MAFR from the EU reform has not entailed a real change. However, due to a longer practice of

MAFR, Italian auditors and audit committee/BSA members were able to provide insights based on their longer experience, about the long-term consequences of such practices. Italian auditors did not express against mandatory rotation, but indicated two main negative consequences, one related to continuous reduction of audit fees and one related with the auditors' learning curve (i.e., time to get to know the client). Such implications from Italy are important to be considered, as they might have impacts later in other EU countries that are new to the MAFR requirements, such as the UK.

4.3.1 Impacts of MAFR on audit quality

In the UK, the MAFR is the greatest change to the UK audit profession out of all the new EU Audit Reforms implemented since 2016. Most auditors, from both Big Four and non-Big Four companies, underlined that the MAFR is clearly new and brings in significant changes in the UK as well as in most European countries. Despite a reasonable expectation that some concerns would have been observed, very little resistance was reported in the UK focus groups. Auditors mainly welcomed the MAFR as an alternative to very long tenure, with positive effects on audit quality:

> *Transition and switching audits are a good thing.*
>
> (Non-Big Four auditor, London, 2018)

> *I think [MAFR] can introduce audit quality in terms of the quality of the intellectual quality and challenge that is brought to an external audit.*
>
> (Non-Big Four auditor, London, 2018)

> *Do I think it was necessarily healthy that some companies had not changed auditor for 50 years? No. So, a degree of change is, yes, I think it's been helpful for external audit quality.*
>
> (Big Four auditor, Edinburgh, 2018)

> *I don't think anybody will say external auditors with the same company for 50 years is a good thing because their viewpoint does become stale […]*
>
> (Professional accounting body, London, 2018)

Having a fresh approach to the audit through the eyes of the new audit firm is generally seen as a positive aspect of the MAFR requirement. Most UK participants agreed that having the same auditor for well over 20 years is not satisfactory, from a perception point of view, and that this audit firm rotation policy is assisting greatly with these perception concerns. The positive aspects that emerged from the interviews and focus groups on MAFR in the UK centre around the elimination of concerns surrounding long tenures, and the advantages of having a "fresh pair of eyes," or a new auditor with a "rethink" or fresh perspective on the audit:

> *I was not in favour of the mandatory tendering, but I think events have shown that it has probably done very little harm and may have done some good when auditors know that they are going to be handing over the audit to another firm.*
>
> (Big Four auditor, London, 2018)

> *Another level, we get both institutions had made in previous years and they're getting most important laws and sometimes people get away from it. I think that certain aspect happens at the audit partner level and at firm level. To the extent that rotation eliminates that is a positive to external audit quality.*
>
> (Non-Big Four auditor, London, 2018)

> *So, a lot of effort's gone into audit tenders. Has that yet improved external audit quality? I suspect it's a little early to say. You always worry that in the year of transition, there's a danger that quality drops because there's a big period of change and new people. Equally, a fresh pair of eyes is incredibly valuable. So, if it helps raise the bar, and if it drives the firms on innovation, particularly around data analytics and things like that, then it'll be a good thing, but I think it's a little early to form a judgement on that.*
>
> (Audit Committee Chair, London, 2019)

Furthermore, there is a view that audit firm rotation does more for eliminating long client-auditor associations and changing the audit approach to any engagement than simply rotating audit partners. While partner rotation was or has been found to be helpful, it is indicated below from some UK participants that audit firm rotation goes further in dealing with these concerns:

> *I think firm rotation is good in many ways. [...] I think there's a perception issue. I think that – whereas rotation of audit partners every five years was helpful, the truth of the matter is that it doesn't really create – or very rarely does it create a radical rethink of the audit. It creates a bit of an evolution maybe, but not a revolution. [...] When you change your auditor, the fact you've got someone coming in, starting with a clean sheet of paper, I think is really, healthy. I think it has – I think it's clearly put more pressure on the audit firms to think about how they define quality. I think they're struggling to do that still. It's quite a difficult thing, but it's made them think much more about that. I think it's engendered some innovation. [...] I'm a big, big fan of tendering.*
>
> (Audit Committee Chair, London, 2018)

> *I do think [audit firm rotation] does send a good message to the public [...] Personally, I don't see it as something which is a key driver of audit quality.*
>
> (Professional accounting body, Edinburgh, 2018)

As expected, participants in Italy indicated that they have long been used to more frequent tenders and their related timing considerations, to be respectful of the Italian rotation requirements. They are convinced that the MAFR requirement of the EU reforms is more of a "trauma" for countries such as Germany and the UK, where auditors have been auditing the same companies for many years:

> *[in] other countries like Germany and the United Kingdom where audited companies used to have the same auditor for 40 to 50 years (Barclays, for example has been audited by the same audit firm for 140 years): in these entities, there has been a real change in the business model, since, before the introduction of this new rule, an auditor would have provided a client with audit services up until retirement.*
>
> (Big Four auditor, Milan, 2018)

While for PIEs the changes in the audit firm rotation are not relevant in Italy, members of the Audit Committee/BSA lament a regulation void regarding large companies that are not publicly listed and thereby not regulated as PIEs. In more detail, in Italy, the capital market is still small, and many large family firms avoid being listed. In this case, audit firms are appointed on a three-year basis, but at the end of the mandate they can be reappointed again and again, without any limitation. Therefore, there is no MAFR for companies that are large (e.g., based on employee numbers, revenues, total assets) but are not listed. In Italy, these types of companies are required to provide a full set of financial statements, which are also compulsorily audited. However, both the domestic Italian and the EU regulations do not require MAFR because these companies are not considered to be PIEs. As a result, they can maintain their auditors if they wish, and for as long as they wish, without any form of control over auditor independence. Furthermore, this is not likely to change any time soon, according to the Italian participants, as far as standardisation of audit regulation and controls is concerned.

Despite a common, favourable general idea on MAFR, in both countries some negative aspects and concerns were reported. Considering their consolidated experience, Italian auditors underlined that the rotation can be costly and time-consuming due to the learning curve issues, especially in large and complex international groups, where new incoming auditors need up to two years to understand the nature, characteristics, and problems of their clients. As a result, the MAFR can have negative implications for the auditors' activities, based on the insights from Italian participants, for the larger multinational clients:

> *The rotation mainly influences groups that are quite complicated. In fact, on one hand, the auditor needs to understand the company he/she works for; on the other hand, he/she also needs to understand both the main issues and the people he/she will have to deal with. [...] It takes auditors nearly two years or more to understand exactly where they are.*
>
> (Big Four auditor, Verona, 2017)

The issue of the loss of knowledge due to auditor rotation is even more pronounced for multinational groups, as auditors of different subsidiaries may be required to rotate at different dates. This may result in a somehow constantly changing audit network, with impacts for both auditors and client firms:

> *Auditors must deal also with issues related to the way their colleagues around the world carry out audit activities. From the auditor's point of view, and even from big groups and clients' point of view, this means losing an investment, losing a report, because they need a setting-in period to understand points of view and needs methods are similar, but they are not the same in each country. And this investment is also partly lost according to the big groups and the clients' point of view.*
>
> (Big Four auditor, Verona, 2017)

In this regard, it is noticeable that in Italy a significant number of consensual resolutions of the audit mandate occurs because of the rotation of the auditor of the parent company's financial statement (29 out of 87 in 2021, 39 out of 68 in 2020; CONSOB, 2021, 2022). Conversely, in very few cases (just 1 in 2021; CONSOB, 2022) the consensual termination is due to the realignment of the mandate to the one of the PIEs pertaining to the same business group.

Among the UK participants, some negative impacts are indicated when referring to the new MAFR from the EU Audit Reform. First, as in the case of opinions raised by Italian auditors, there are concerns about learning curve issues and costs in the provision of an audit to a new client in the UK. There are concerns regarding audit quality during the first two years of a new audit, as auditors are on a steep learning curve. However, beyond the first two years, there is less concern, as auditors usually have already gained a good understanding of the client's business and its operating environment. On this point, among several auditors' opinions, the following is particularly relevant:

> *I'm a supporter of change, of transitions, but the counterview is, in my experience, that it takes you two years at least to get up to speed*

on the audit. If you're taking on a huge audit, the first year you may have all the processes in place and tick all the boxes, but you weren't necessarily getting underneath all the stones that you need to, in that first year and probably not even in the second year. So, my experience, by the third year, you pretty well know the business by then.

(Non-Big Four auditor, London, 2018)

Second, various participants highlighted they believe that existing regulations already provided by UK laws (prior to the 2014 EU Audit Reform) was sufficient to guarantee an appropriate level of auditor independence, and thus audit quality. The reference is, of course, to partner rotation, which had been in effect for more than a decade in the UK and was still supported among several UK auditors and, likewise, the professional bodies in the UK. The following comment is particularly indicative of the view the latter shared during one focus group:

We [a professional accounting body] argued against it [firm rotation] when we were going through the commentary process with the EU, partly because from an independence point of view, we think that it's already dealt with by the existing UK laws on personnel, such as audit partner rotation, fee dependency issues and all that stuff.

(Professional accounting body, London, 2018)

Because of the extent of the change, it is not surprising that more controversial opinions were raised during interviews. Organisational aspects were mentioned by the auditors, as well as their relationship with the employees of the audited company and the perceptions of external stakeholders on auditor independence and audit quality, meaning that auditing is not regarded as a stand-alone activity but is embedded in society. A few citations are reported below, which offer interesting insights on the various faces of auditing as a social practice:

[After a few years] you know the people who you can trust, the people who tend to give you a flippant answer hoping you'll go away, you know the areas that concern the business because "they keep cropping up, and so you've got a real insight, so you can shape your audit and your audit-thinking as a partner, your risk management is much better, whereas in the first year, it's a huge on boarding of information. You go through the process, you apply all the audit statistical sampling, etcetera but this is far from a real comprehend and just know what doesn't look right. It's not as strong as in two years' time. So, there is a risk in changing audits but, overall, I think it's a good thing [...]."

(Non-Big Four, London, 2018)

> *[...] there is that threat that some of these organizations are complex and some of them are very complex. And getting to grips, the auditor gets to grips with systems, with judgments, even the take on senior management and knowing where the risks are, that's not easy, and there's a bit of a learning curve. I think we've got better over years because I think if you go to a large company tender and you win that tender, what tends to happen is you've got this shadow year where you don't go cold and what you tend to do is shadow the previous audit for a year and I think that helps safeguard audit quality from the learning curve perspective. So, I think [...] firm rotation has both positives and negatives. But I think the one thing it does do is my close observation is there's a perception that the familiarly with auditors and their clients and I think mandatory firm rotation to the extent that addresses that, enhances the confidence, and uses that in the quality audits. So, again, it goes back to that confidence.*
>
> (Non-Big Four auditor, London, 2018)

Last, but not the least, some UK participants raised some comments "out of the chorus" that deserve particular attention. One Big Four auditor commented on contingent factors that have helped – or even replaced – the EU reform improve audit quality:

> *I think it [the EU reform] has improved audit quality and I think it's also coincided with technology and innovation or more options around innovation. [...] in today's world of rigorous independent oversight and the oversight bodies are in our office all the time may have their own room, and in a world where you're competing on quality, the audit quality results around in public. Audit committees are feeling it and you can't afford to get it wrong. So, I would say if you thought about XXX [anonymous case], we took that over probably one of those complex external audits there is. [...] we've probably done the best audits ever in the first couple of years because you can't afford to get it wrong.*
>
> (Big Four auditor, London, 2018)

A member of a professional body highlighted possible implications of the introduction of MAFR on the audit firms' overall strategy and business model:

> *[w]hat's [MAFR] done is it generated more competition amongst auditors in terms of innovation, to think how auditors confess to differentiate themselves and how they can remain profitable and effective when audit is no longer – you're not pointed as an auditor and remain there for maybe 20 or 30 years, and lots of rules around mandatory rotation*

> *and service of the independence, to improve in the independence of auditors and therefore limitations as to what further services can be provided.*
>
> (Regulator, London, 2018)

In his turn, a member of another professional body invited to think about the matters of fact that, first, the personnel of both auditee companies and audit firms change over time and, second, the engagement partner is always under pressure, with or without an MAFR rule in place:

> *And also, I can see that from a tradition point of view, if you're a firm that's had a particular entity as your audit client for 60–70 years, that to challenge them and stand up to them with the risk of potentially losing them might be seen as a stain on the reputation of the engagement partner in that case. So, I could see that having a mechanism that says they're going to go off 20 years, come what may, allows the engagement partners to be independent and to stand up where he needs to stand up because he doesn't have that pressure of, "I can't be the one to lose this one for the firm."*
>
> (Professional accounting body, London, 2018)

Overall, several, differentiated opinions emerged during the interviews on the effects of MAFR on audit quality, both in the UK and in Italy. The learning curve that newly appointed auditors shall go through and the changeable audit network in large multinational group where companies are subject to different tenure/rotation requirement are mentioned as the main shortcomings of MAFR by Italian auditors, considering their long-standing experience. UK auditors especially raised criticism on the incremental benefit of MAFR over audit partner rotation and look forward to assessing the impacts – if any – of the new requirement. A common stand is found in that perceptions of all the participants in the UK and Italy ranged from positive to doubtful, but no evident negative perception was expressed.

4.3.2 Impacts of MAFR on audit costs and audit fees

Among the UK participants, several concerns were expressed around the potential increase of the tendering costs. In detail, early views gathered in 2017 and 2018 suggest that UK participants were already forecasting what had already happened in Italy after over 40 years of MAFR. The implementation costs of audit firm rotation, such as the tendering process and the initial years of learning the processes and business of a new audit client, are predicted to continue to increase in the UK. The learning curve costs are typically borne by the audit firms; however, these costs over time would be passed back onto the clients via audit fees, thus increasing the costs of statutory audits to the wider society in general. Among several auditors' opinions on this point, the following are particularly relevant:

> *The cost of tendering is huge in terms of the audit market here in the UK, like to get to know the strategy plans of a new client and then go through various standards and produce thorough documentation for a new client.*
>
> (Big Four auditor, London, 2018)

> *Firms will be forced to incur the costs of participating in audit tenders that they may not have much chance of winning. Choices also need to be made about whether firms wish to provide audit or non-audit services to clients – choices that may be very difficult to change if circumstances later change.*
>
> (CFO, Edinburgh, 2018)

Other critical aspects reported as regards tendering are related to its timing, the effort it requires, and the expectations in respect to Big Four audit firms. All such aspects are mentioned below in a very effective way:

> *Tendering processes, I think it's perhaps being a bit detrimental toward equality, the reason being that [...] what constant audit tendering has done is taking away focus and investment at the time when the audit firms could've been investing in better audit technology, better audit techniques, better analytics. Much of that investment has gone into trying to retender sometimes for audits which they would not and will not win, but where the market expects them to compete. [...] even within the Big four, many of the tenders that they participated, they don't expect to win, but they still must take all the investment, which is very, very substantial for a global audit to tender, and therefore that has taken away from a potential investment on audit quality. [...] I don't necessarily think a seven-year cycle is positive. In the end, they compromise position of the EU with the ten-year and 20-year. Once you get into those kinds of fixed periods, I'm not sure any of that is particularly advantageous.*
>
> (Big Four auditor, Edinburgh, 2018)

Assuming a different perspective, some participants from Big Four companies came to minimise the organisational impact of MAFR in the UK. See, for instance, the following thought:

> *I suspect it of the points of view of auditors and corporate, it's just something they will have to be managed. It's something we cover with big impact – initially a pain but it's something that can be managed. I don't see that having particularly dramatic consequences.*
>
> (Big Four auditor, London, 2018)

Given their proven experience with MAFR, Italian auditors provided insights on its long-term consequences, which indicate some negative impacts. These may be very important considerations for EU regulators to consider, to help in avoiding any such negative consequences for the audit profession in Europe. There are two main negative long-term consequences that Italian auditors indicated to us in this study. First, after every audit firm rotation, the audit fee is generally said to reduce by 20%–30%, while the continuous change in regulations requires additional effort that is not adequately remunerated by the audit and assurance market. At the same time, the change of audit firm is also an additional cost for the auditee. This is not seen as a good thing for maintaining or improving audit quality:

> *Every time an auditor changes according to the rotation policy, our remuneration [audit fee] decreases by around 20–30%.*
>
> (Big Four auditor, Verona, 2018)

> *[T]he rotation of the audit firm has only helped to reduce fees. [...] the fact of changing audit firms has only generated price wars [...].*
>
> (Big Four auditor, Verona, 2017)

In summary, much concern is expressed on the impact of MAFR on the overall costs of the audit activity, for both auditors and client firms. On the one hand, needless forcing is especially perceived by UK auditors and managers as regards taken-for-granted participation into tendering processes which will be lost since the very beginning. On the other hand, Italian auditors report their low-balling experience to win tenders, which brings a continuous reduction of the audit revenues at the beginning of a new mandate. Moreover, additional costs shall be faced when taking a new mandate and because of the frequent change in regulation. Combining such dynamics, which tend to impact the audit client as well, the position of auditors on the effects of MAFR on audit fees is quite adverse.

4.3.3 Impacts of MAFR on market concentration

One of the main reasons why the EU introduced the MAFR is to promote competition in the audit market, thus reducing market concentration levels and incentivising participation of smaller companies to PIEs' audit tenders. The audit market data is impressive: before Regulation 537/2014 became effective, in the EU less than 6% of the total number of registered audit firms were carrying out statutory audits of PIEs (1,742 over 32,306 in 2015). While Italy was aligned with such a percentage, in the UK the situation was even more worrying, as less than 1% of the total number of registered audit firms were engaged in statutory audits of PIEs (50 over 6,331). The number of statutory audits completed by such audit firms was huge: in 2015, throughout the EU, 1,742 audit firms covered almost

30,000 audits of PIEs (on average, 17 per audit firm), in the UK 50 audit firms performed 1,748 audits of PIEs (on average, 35 per audit firm), and in Italy 26 audit firms were engaged in 1,578 audits of PIEs' accounts (on average, 61 per audit firm). Moreover, the Big Four held a concentrated oligopoly in terms of both the number of statutory audits of PIEs and turnover (EC, 2017).

Despite the EU Audit Reform, in the UK, market concentration remains a concern for all the stakeholders interviewed. Indeed, although the tender process is seen as very competitive, investors, audit committee members, and professional accounting bodies all share the belief that such mandatory rotation would maintain the current levels of Big Four dominance in the UK audit market:

> *[...] it will take a few years, but I think they've solved the problem of long tenure, that means more switching, but in terms of switching to what, it's just concentrated things even further. I mean the Big Four still are concentrated.*
>
> (Investor, London, 2018)

> *[MAFR] hasn't opened competition in this country, but it has made the Big Four more competitive amongst themselves.*
>
> (Audit Committee Chair, London, 2018)

> *[MAFR] doesn't seem to have done anything for competition – certainly in terms of concentration rather than competition.*
>
> (Professional accounting body, London, 2018)

The idea emerged that the Big Four have been dominant for years and that everything that has happened in the world, e.g., globalisation, has made them and will continue to make them more and more dominant.

When dealing with MAFR and audit market concentration, the opinion of non-Big Four auditors is key. In the UK, mixed perceptions were expressed: some auditors share – and are worrying about – the idea that competition has especially increased among the Big Four. An impression is also expressed that non-Big Four auditors might not be interested in entering that competition, or not have enough resources to enter the latter:

> *So, all that's happened quite frankly is that's that deck cards have been shuffled. [...] If you're saying the idea of the [...] EU conclusions around audit regulation was to bring in greater competition, well they only brought great competition amongst the four firms, they didn't introduce, and wouldn't introduce through that process. We said it in time wouldn't introduce new players.*
>
> (Non-Big Four auditor, London, 2018)

> *The people who were speculating that there was insufficient competition between the Big Four, they'd surely have to acknowledge that there has been therefore an increase in competition between the Big Four, because of that tendering. [...] if the objective was only to break outside of the Big Four then it has not achieved any result. But the counter argument to that is, do the non-Big Four firms want to take the investment too in those jobs? And that's questionable.*
>
> (Non-Big Four auditor, Edinburgh, 2018)

> *[n]ow we're finding that firms outside the Big Four are finding the tender process expensive, particularly expensive if you don't ever win.*
>
> (Professional accounting body, London, 2018)

Assuming a different viewpoint, another concern relates to the willingness of large, listed companies to invite non-Big Four audit firms to the tendering process. Such a concern was expressed by non-Big Four auditors and confirmed in different interviews by audit committee members:

> *I think it depends on how many companies are willing to make sure they invite non-Big Four Firms to tender for their audits of large, listed companies.*
>
> (Non-Big Four auditor, London, 2018)

> *[...] even on our FTSE 150, when that's tendered [...] I started off saying, we'll have the Big Four there. We took – as we – when we took a closer look, just didn't have the scale, didn't have the sector experience, so we – so I don't know the solution to that.*
>
> (Audit Committee Chair, London, 2018)

Despite all such concerns, some non-Big Four auditors look at the reform with a more positive attitude and recognise that the MAFR created new opportunities for non-Big Four audit firms:

> *For me, it makes a series of good points. For me, it's certainly from our sector we're resilient organizations and you can cope with a lot of stuff, and I would say that's something that creates people to rethink what they're doing every few years almost certainly has benefits. If there are dangers in policymakers who are saying nothing has changed, be it competition or quality or whatever it is, so I've got to make very radical changes, so you're forcing people to make very radical changes or doing it very quickly such as you're bringing in regulation very quickly or you're having a mandatory rotation or tendering for very short periods.*
>
> (Non-Big Four auditor, London, 2019)

In Italy, focus groups and interviews did not delve much into market concentration. Indeed, despite MAFR being in place since 1975, the level of market concentration in favour of the Big Four has always been very high. According to the most recent data published by CONSOB (2021), 25 audit firms conduct audit activities for around 1,400 PIEs. This data does not show any significant improvement of the situation existing before the EU Audit Reform was enforced: indeed, in 2015 each audit firm oversaw 61 statutory audits of PIEs (EC, 2017) and in 2021 the average was still 56 audits (Kend et al., 2021). The percentage of listed companies whose financial statements are audited by one of the Big Four firms ranged from 88% to 91% in the period 2015–2020. In 2021, the Big Four owned 198 mandates, equal to 90% market share. Medium- and small-sized audit firms were responsible for the auditing of 12 and 8 annual reports, respectively (CONSOB, 2021). In 2015, the European Commission (EC) qualified Italy as a country where the Big Four companies held a concentrated oligopoly in terms of turnover (EC, 2017). No changes are foreseeable soon, thus confirming that audit market concentration, and in particular the dominance of the Big Four, remains a matter of concern in the country.

4.4 Summary

In summary, the views on the MAFR and its impacts on auditors' activities and organisational practices were mixed across Italy and in the UK. First, the change generally had opposite reactions: it is defined as quite radical by UK participants, whilst it is "nothing new" for Italian participants. Positive impacts are indicated by UK participants, especially in terms of the importance of having "fresh eyes" in the auditing process. However, both Italy and the UK indicate similar negative impacts regarding the tendering process cost increases and the learning curve issues. This is particularly interesting if one considers that what UK participants indicated as negative impacts immediately after the EU Audit Reform (2014) are impacts that Italy has been lamenting for the past 45 years. This is a very important aspect that EU regulators should consider. Indeed, our findings confirm that the perceived benefits of MAFR in terms of audit quality might be offset by negative effects of the huge efforts required and costs incurred for the tendering process and in the first years of any new engagement. Moreover, such negative effects are not limited to the period immediately after the change but tend to affect the audit clients – and the society more in general – also in the long run. EU regulators should monitor such consequences, especially when these are the results of a generalised regulatory reform imposed on several EU countries for the sake of auditors' independence.

Finally, despite the good intentions of the EU to encourage participation by non-Big Four audit firms for the audit tenders of PIEs and thus reduce audit market concentration, both UK and Italian interviewees expressed many concerns on the MAFR potential to really go in that direction. For several reasons that span from the resources available to the Big and non-Big Four, the willingness of the non-Big Four to tender, and the willingness of audit clients to invite the non-Big Four to tender, the perception is that market concentration may continue to increase, and competition may become higher and higher just among the Big Four audit companies. And latest data goes exactly in such a direction. The CMA report (2018) indicated that when it came to tenders, some smaller practitioners were not considered to have the capability or "global footprint," and thus were precluded from the invitation to tender. The solution then could be that Big Four and non-Big Four firms arrange joint or shared audits which will assist in the sharing of fees in the UK and in the building of the expertise and help to acquire more experience for smaller practitioners.

References

Allam, A., Ghattas, N., Kotb, A., and Khaled Eldaly, M. (2017). Audit tendering in the UK: A review of stakeholders' views. *International Journal of Auditing*, 21(1): 11–23. https://doi.org/10.1111/ijau.12076

Aschauer, E., and Quick, R. (2018). Mandatory audit firm rotation and prohibition of audit firm provided tax services: Evidence from investment consultants' perceptions. *International Journal of Auditing*, 22: 131–149. https://doi.org/10.1111/ijau.12109

Aziz, U., and Omoteso, K. (2014). Reinforcing users' confidence in statutory audit during a post-crisis period. An empirical study. *Journal of Applied Accounting Research*, 15(3): 308–322. https://doi.org/10.1108/JAAR-11-2013-0108

Cameran, M., Francis, J., Marra, A., and Pettinicchio, A. (2015). Are there adverse consequences of mandatory auditor rotation? Evidence from the Italian experience. *Auditing: A Journal of Practice & Theory*, 34(1): 1–24. https://doi.org/10.2308/ajpt-50663

Commonwealth of Australia (2002). Corporate Law Economic Reform Program Proposals for Reform (CLERP): Discussion Paper No. 9. Corporate Disclosure: Strengthening the Financial Reporting Framework, September.

Competition & Market Authority—CMA (2018). *Statutory audit services market study*. London: National Archives.

CONSOB (Commissione Nazionale per le Società e la Borsa), Relazione per l'anno 2020, Roma, 31 marzo (2021). ISSN 2282-1392 (online). Available at: https://www.consob.it/documents/46180/46181/rel2020.pdf/bf6c875a-b0fd-429b-b585-86fd651995af. Accessed 19.04.22.

CONSOB (Commissione Nazionale per le Società e la Borsa), Relazione per l'anno 2021, Roma, 31 marzo (2022). ISSN 2282-1392 (online). Available at: https://www.consob.it/documents/46180/46181/ra2021.pdf/5da5eda5-85a9-464b-8e08-944e462aec33. Accessed 19.04.22.

Corbella, S., Florio, C., Gotti, G., and Mastrolia, S. (2015). Audit firm rotation, audit fees, and audit quality: The experience of Italian public companies. *Journal of International Accounting, Auditing and Taxation*, 25: 46–66.

Ewelt-Knauer, C., Gold, A., and Pott, C. (2013). Mandatory audit firm rotation: A review of stakeholder perspectives and prior research. *Accounting in Europe*, 10(1): 27–41. https://doi.org/10.1080/17449480.2013.772717

European Commission (2017). Report on monitoring developments in the EU market for providing statutory audit services to public-interest entities pursuant to Article 27 of Regulation (EU) 537/2014.

European Union (2014). Regulation (EU) No 537/2014 of the European parliament and of the council of 16 April 2014 on specific requirements regarding statutory audit of public-interest entities and repealing Commission Decision 2005/909/EC. Available at: http://eur-lex.europa.eu/legal-content/EN/TXT/PDF/?uri=CELEX:32014R0537&from=EN. Accessed 19.03.22.

FRC (2016). The UK Corporate Governance Code.

Garcia-Blandon, J., Argiles-Bosch, J., Castillo-Merino, D., and Martinez-Blasco, M. (2017). An assessment of the provisions of regulation (EU) No 537/2014 on non-audit services and audit firm tenure: Evidence from Spain. *The International Journal of Accounting,* 52(3): 251–261. https://doi.org/10.1016/j.intacc.2017.07.003

Garcia-Blandon, J., Argiles-Bosch, J., and Ravenda, D. (2020). Audit firm tenure and audit quality: A cross-European study. *Journal of International Financial Management & Accounting,* 31(1): 35–64. https://doi.org/10.1111/jifm.12098

Government Accounting Office (GAO) (2003). Report to the senate committee on banking, housing, and urban affairs, and the house committee on financial services. In Public accounting firms: Required study on the potential effects of mandatory audit firm rotation. November report.

Hohenfels, D. (2016). Auditor tenure and perceived earnings quality. *International Journal of Auditing,* 20(3): 224–238. https://doi.org/10.1111/ijau.12069

Jackson, A., Moldrich, M., and Roebuck, P. (2008). Mandatory audit firm rotation and audit quality. *Managerial Auditing Journal,* 23(5): 420–437. https://doi.org/10.1108/02686900810875271

Kend, M., Leoni, G., Florio, C., and Gaia, S. (2021). *EU audit reforms: Analysing different impacts in the UK and Italy.* London: ICAEW.

Myers, J., Myers, L., and Omer, T. (2003). Exploring the term of the auditor-client relationship and the quality of earnings: A case for mandatory auditor rotation? *The Accounting Review,* 78: 779–799. https://doi.org/10.2308/accr.2003.78.3.779

Polychronidou, P., Drogalas, G., and Tampakoudis, I. (2020). Mandatory rotation of audit firms and auditors in Greece. *International Journal of Disclosure and Governance,* 17: 141–154. https://doi.org/10.1057/s41310-020-00080-3

Public Company Accounting Oversight Board (PCAOB) (2011). Concept release on auditor independence and audit firm rotation. Concept Release (no. 39).

Ruhnke, K., and Schmidt, M. (2014). The audit expectation gap: Existence, causes, and the impact of changes. *Accounting and Business Research,* 44(5): 572–601. https://doi.org/10.1080/00014788.2014.929519

Sarbanes-Oxley Act of 2002, PL 107-204, 116 Stat 745.

Taminiau, Y., and Heusinkveld, S. (2017). Role expectations and agency in the audit tendering process. *Accounting, Auditing & Accountability Journal,* 30(8): 1820–1842. https://doi.org/10.1108/AAAJ-10-2015-2258

5 Restrictions and caps on non-audit work

Challenges and response strategies

5.1 Introduction

This chapter contains a comparative analysis of the EU (European Union) Audit Reform's impacts in both the UK and Italy, by examining restrictions and caps on non-audit services (NAS). Within this chapter, we also examine and discuss issues related to the adjustments to internal quality controls within audit firms, and audit processes and strategies, and recalibrations to audit firms' risk management systems and structures, in response to such changes. The EU Audit Reform has introduced specific restrictions on a range of NAS that public interest entities (PIEs) in the EU can obtain from the audit firm and its network. The restrictions apply to the period between the beginning of the period audited and the issuing of the audit report, as well as to the financial year immediately preceding the period audited. As conveyed in Chapter 1, with a few Member States' exceptions, the NAS that are prohibited by the 2014 EU Audit Reform are the following:

1. certain tax services.
2. services that involve playing any part in the management or decision-making of the audited entity.
3. bookkeeping and preparing accounting records and financial statements.
4. designing and implementing internal control or risk management procedures related to the preparation and/or control of financial information or designing and implementing financial information technology systems.
5. certain valuation services (e.g., performed in connection with actuarial or litigation support services).
6. certain legal services.
7. services related to the audited entity's internal audit function.
8. services linked to the financing, capital structure and allocation, and investment strategy of the audited entity.
9. promoting, dealing in, or underwriting shares in the audited entity.
10. payroll and other human resources services.

DOI: 10.4324/9781003262596-5

Typically, when major reforms such as these in the EU are proposed or implemented accounting research studies focus on the benefits and costs (Houghton et al., 2013). For instance, Ruhnke and Schmidt (2016) analysed the expected benefits and costs associated with five potential changes to the institutional framework of statutory audits in Europe. These proposals had been first published in the EU in 2010 and, after extensive debate, revised and adopted by the EU Council of Ministers consisting of a directive and a regulation in April 2014 (as discussed above). In another research, Lombardi et al. (2021) found that the EU Directive fostered changes to large public companies' reporting practices and external pressures contributed to influencing changes to internal organisational practices in terms of new internal processes, procedures, and structures.

5.2 Auditor's independence and the restrictions and caps on NAS

5.2.1 Audit independence

An auditor is required to be independent from the entity it audits. The joint provision of NAS and audit services has been viewed as a potential threat to auditor independence by regulators in the EU. The independence requirements applying to auditors are legally enforceable in many EU Member States. However, there are some professionals such as the Institute of Chartered Accountants in England and Wales (ICAEW) that suggest a blanket prohibition on the provision of NAS to audit clients can be inefficient for the client and is neither necessary to ensure independence nor helpful in contributing to the knowledge necessary to ensure the quality of the audit (ICAEW, 2022). Assuming no undue overall economic dependence results from the auditor/client relationship and adequate safeguards can be implemented, the ICAEW believes that companies themselves should determine whether they use external auditors for NAS, in consultation with the profession's guidelines (ICAEW, 2022). The ICAEW has been concerned that unnecessarily restricting the provision of NAS would have an unintended, adverse effect on the underlying quality of the audit through restrictions in knowledge and skills (ICAEW, 2022). So, clearly there are several aspects to the debate, and while we do not detail all the issues within this chapter, we acknowledge that restricting NAS has its benefits and disadvantages.

Maintaining independence has several aspects that the external auditor must be mindful of throughout the client/auditor relationship. Like members of many other professions, however, external auditors often face challenges to their independence. Many challenges arise because external auditors are hired, paid, and even fired by the organisations that they audit rather than by the people they presumably represent. Ultimately, if external audit appointments and fees are determined by the company being audited, the external auditor can never truly be economically independent of the client. That is why there are broader codes of professional conduct for both auditors and accountants which govern the relationship between both parties (auditor and client). A brief overview of the areas an auditor must be aware of and implement appropriate responses in include: (i) conflict of interest situations (which include threats like self-interest and self-review); and (ii) diligence by external auditors in identifying and evaluating threats to independence and applying appropriate safeguards. Auditor independence is part of the foundation of the auditing profession; it is like the cornerstone of the profession. An independent, reliable, and ethically sound financial statement audit gives a public company credibility and allows investors and potential investors to trust in the accuracy of the results and the integrity of the accounting profession more generally. Audit firm size appears to be the most important factor that affects the auditor independence, followed by tenure, competition, audit committee, audit firms providing NAS, and size of audit fee. The "self-review" threat is considered one of the most serious threats to auditor independence. We discuss more about self-review threats and how they are relevant to the audit independence risks associated with the joint provision of NAS and audit services below. Next, we consider some of the relevant audit literature that has considered the caps and restrictions on NAS due to the 2014 EU audit directive.

5.2.2 Literature on the restrictions and caps on NAS

Ruhnke and Schmidt (2016) surveyed a broad range of listed and unlisted companies in Germany and found that respondents viewed none of the proposed changes as associated with any (net) benefit. The incremental costs of these EU Audit Reforms were expected to exceed the incremental benefits. Their study was limited to just management and board representatives from auditees, and they suggest future research investigate the perceptions of other stakeholder groups (i.e., auditors and regulators would be essential). In a study focused on the Austrian setting, Aschauer and Quick (2018) provide experimental evidence on the effects of the prohibition of audit firm-provided tax services and the interplay of such measure with the provision of mandatory auditor rotation as perceived by professional consultants from credit institutions. The prohibition against tax services is found to improve perceived auditor independence and audit quality, but neither independence nor audit quality improves further when such prohibition is also combined with the implementation of mandatory audit firm rotation. Another study, Horton et al. (2018), focused on investigating investors' perceptions of these EU regulatory changes to audit in Europe. While investors did not appear to react significantly to the mandatory rotation proposals, they did react positively and significantly to the restriction of NAS and the capping of total fees. Their study partially offset the doubts Ratzinger-Sakel and Schönberger (2015) expressed on the efficiency and effectiveness of EU restrictions on NAS. By analysing data available on NAS in France,

Germany, and the UK, they found that, even before the EU reform, in audit practice the volume of NAS provided to the largest PIEs was largely below the cap provided for by the EU Regulation. Therefore, Ratzinger-Sakel and Schönberger (2015) concluded that EU reform on NAS "might prevent potential concerns of impaired auditor independence but may affect the current audit market only partially" (p. 62). Moreover, they question the EU reform potential for audit quality improvement, due to "lost knowledge spill overs from newly banned NAS" (p. 62).

This debate regarding NAS provision and restrictions has not only been prevalent in the EU; in fact, it has been widespread for many decades around the world. The effect of auditor-provided NAS on audit quality has been a long-standing and globally widespread debate among academics, practitioners, and regulators (Beardsley et al., 2021). Payments for NAS by client firms can impair auditor independence and motivate auditors to ignore audit client deficiencies (Friedman and Mahieux, 2021). Regulators such as the PCAOB in the US are concerned that over-emphasising NAS relative to the audit can divert resources away from the audit function and push personnel to subordinate the external audit function to other business lines (Beardsley et al., 2021). For example, a greater overall emphasis on business lines other than the external audit function would result in lower investments in technology, innovation, and training for the audit practice of a firm (Beardsley et al., 2021). These actions can reduce audit quality for all firm clients, not just those purchasing high levels of NAS (Beardsley et al., 2021). However, the provision of NAS to audit clients may improve auditor's ability to detect material misstatements through knowledge spill-overs (Friedman and Mahieux, 2021). From a theoretical point of view, the joint provision of audit and NAS exerts opposing effects on audit quality, and the overall impact remains unclear and is still open to debate (Quick, 2022). Empirical evidence on the impact of NAS prohibition on audit quality is still scant. A notable exception is Garcia-Blandon et al. (2017), who collected data on Spanish listed companies. Their results do not suggest lower audit quality when NAS and audit services are jointly provided to the same client firm. Such finding is confirmed also when fees for NAS overcome the limit of 70% of audit fees fixed by the EU Audit Reform (2014), when the audit firm provides tax-related NAS, audit-related NAS, or other NAS to audit clients.

5.3 Restrictions and caps on NAS in the UK and Italy

As a way of introduction, it is useful to clarify that while Italian firms fully comply with the EU NAS restrictions, UK audit firms can continue to provide certain tax and valuation services to their clients. Moreover, audit firms in both countries are now subject to fee caps for NAS provided to audit clients, in that the EU Audit Reform (2014) requires that the total fees for NAS be limited to no more than 70% of the average of the fees paid in the last three consecutive financial years for the statutory audit(s) of the audited company.

Over several years, market participants have viewed the NAS provision as a zero-sum game. However, interestingly, the markets for audit and NAS in the UK and Italy are sensibly different. The 2018 CMA report based on the UK market shows that the Big Four derive substantially more revenue from NAS than they do from audits. Across the Big Four as a whole, NAS in the UK accounted for 79% of total revenues in 2018 (a slight increase from 77% in 2011). Revenues earned on NAS exceed by a factor of four those earned on audit services in the UK (CMA, 2018). NAS is a large business for most of the major audit firms, so it would be no surprise if auditors are concerned about the possibility of restrictions on the joint provision of audit and NAS. Conversely, Cameran and Santoli (2018) show that, in Italy, the Big Four are providing more and more NAS, yet in 2017 revenues from NAS equalled just 20% of total revenues (with a significant increase from 8% in 2013). The proportion between audit and NAS is thus opposite to that in the UK. Below are the main views from participants on having NAS restrictions and auditors providing NAS to audit clients. An EC report (EC, 2017) shows that, on average, 35% of the EU turnover of audit firms auditing PIEs originated from audit-related activities (i.e., statutory audit of PIEs, of entities belonging to a group of undertakings whose parent undertaking is a PIE and of other entities). Therefore, around two-thirds of the EU turnover of audit firms auditing PIEs originated from NAS revenues gained by delivering both permitted NAS to audited entities (14% of overall turnover) and NAS to other (non-audited) entities (51% of the overall turnover). Combining the evidence from the various reports available, Italy and the UK are interesting cases to investigate as they are positioned at the two opposite extremes of revenue generation in Europe when partitioning between audit services and NAS. The following sub-sections examine various issues that have emerged due to the restrictions on NAS imposed by the EU Audit Reform (2014) and how these reforms impact Italy and the UK differently.

5.3.1 Impacts and changes to auditors' market strategy

The comparative analysis of the EU Audit Reform's impacts in the UK and Italy has shed light on the perceived impacts of restrictions and caps on NAS by UK and Italian audit practitioners.

In the UK, the introduction of restrictions on NAS has pushed audit firms to make strategic decisions and to prioritise the NAS provision to large companies rather than take on low margin audits. Some PIEs are adopting the approach of using two of the firms for NAS and keeping a third firm relatively "clean" in case they need to change auditors. This effectively means that a company has a choice of one when it needs to change auditors from the incumbent auditor. Thus, while audit firms are searching for the more lucrative NAS work as a priority to new audit work, clients are negotiating the fine balance between maintaining audit independence and having enough auditor choice when it comes to audit tendering.

> *You are starting to see already some Big Four firms bullied by big companies to compete for their audit tenders because they prefer to maintain their audit independence leading to other consulting work. I know of one big company, that had to tell one of the Big Four firms, "If you do not bid for the audit, we will never give you any further consulting work."*
>
> (Big Four auditor, London, 2018)

In many cases, auditors must now reduce their existing level of NAS work to take on audit clients because of the auditor independence rules and the desire to avoid any perception of conflict. This is also confirmed by the CMA report (2018), which provides limited evidence of conflicts between audit and NAS work at the client level, primarily because of the restrictions in place on cross-selling. The CMA report (2018) indicates that audit firms typically provide NAS to audit clients well below the 70% cap imposed by the EU Audit Reform (2014) in the UK. There has long been debate on addressing shareholder concerns regarding the independence of auditors and the provision of NAS to audit clients. The provision of NAS reduces auditor independence, which may decrease audit quality and in turn render undesirable the provision of NAS by auditors. However, some argue that the joint provision does not impair an auditor's independence. Instead, it reduces total costs, enhances the ability to detect material misstatements, increases technical competence due to knowledge spill-overs, and leads to intense market competition. Balanced against the need for auditors to remain profitable with viable business models and maintaining audit quality, this debate is ongoing with no easy solution.

A study by Kend and Nguyen (2022) focused on better understanding the interactions between external auditors, their audit clients and audit regulators, when considering the supply of and demand for high-level audit technology. Through the theoretical lens of the socio-technical systems of innovation theory, their study involved semi-structured interviews with 25 stakeholders in Australia and New Zealand during 2019–2020, and 21 stakeholders in the UK during 2016–2017. Kend and Nguyen (2022) reported that this technological demand is driven not only by audit clients and their technologies, but also originally by consultancy (non-audit) services. External auditors have access to large quantities of their clients' data (from both consulting and audit work); thus, they can provide value-adding business insights for their audit clients (Kend and Nguyen, 2022). External auditors viewed the provision of these analytics-based business insights to justify maintaining or increasing audit fees and to mitigate audit fee conflicts (Austin et al., 2021). When processing information, some respondents in the UK from the Kend and Nguyen (2022) study even went as far as revealing that the primary pressures for more audit data analytics (ADA) were in fact driven by NAS.

The UK regulator, the Financial Reporting Council (FRC) (2020a), stated that some emerging technologies, such as machine learning and predictive analysis, although largely at a research stage, present further opportunities to improve audit quality but also raise challenges for both audit firms and audit regulators in terms of compliance with audit standards (Kend and Nguyen, 2022). The FRC (UK) (2020b) stated that a key challenge for the audit profession is to ensure that auditing standards remain fit for purpose, setting objectives and requirements for auditors which are designed to ensure consistent delivery of high-quality audits, whilst allowing for innovation and deployment of increasingly sophisticated technological resources. Therefore, the pressures for more ADA services which are driven by NAS also have unintended consequences for audit quality and the relevance of auditing standards. Relevant audit research, for example, Christ et al. (2021) who interviewed national-level partners and audit standard setters, highlights impediments to adopting these technologies, including audit firm concerns about being first movers combined with the inability of audit standard setters to provide guidance at a pace that matches the pace of technological development. With many of the existing auditing standards still referring to audit sampling, updating standards to support the evolving technology is crucial; otherwise, there are detection risks related to auditors not being guided sufficiently in testing entire populations (Kend and Nguyen, 2020). Studies such as Christ et al. (2021) and Kend and Nguyen (2022) acknowledge that keeping up with the pace of change is a major challenge for audit regulators and standard setters. Salijeni et al. (2019) found that external auditors perceive a lack of guidance from auditing standards as an opportunity to innovate without worrying about possibly substantial regulatory restrictions. However, participants in Kend and Nguyen (2022) challenge these findings by Salijeni et al. (2019), in that external auditors should refrain from fully engaging with new audit technologies, unless the auditing standard setters eliminate what they see as uncertainties around ADA usage. We further discuss these issues around ADA technology and standard setting in Chapter 7.

Non-Big Four auditors have invested significantly less in ADA technologies, thus indicating a widening of the gap between the larger and smaller practitioners (Kend and Nguyen, 2022). If shared audits are introduced in the UK as proposed in the CMA report (2018), then future research should investigate the sharing of technological resources by the larger and smaller audit firms, as they would be required to conduct audits together under the proposal. This proposed audit reform may reverse the trend of this widening gap between the larger and smaller practitioners (Kend and Nguyen, 2022). In Section 5.2.2 we further discuss these impacts on the smaller practitioners. So, although pressures remain on external auditors to maintain profitable business models and continue to adopt innovative emerging technologies, perception issues persist and finding the right balance in the joint provision of audit and NAS will always be difficult. Managing this internally within audit firms has been vital, although only a few UK interview participants discussed the importance of this matter, whereas Italian respondents (see findings below) highlight the stricter authorisation processes related to NAS provision in Italy:

> *So, we do not think that you need to have a model which restricts large amounts of non-audit services, so the real big issue is perception. The smaller issue, but only a bit smaller, is whether you can manage the independence and objectivity internally.*
>
> (UK standard setter, London, 2018)

> *I think the economics is one round and audits are getting so much less and less attractive. But the issue for the Big Four firm is deciding what to give up.*
>
> (Big Four auditor, London, 2018)

In Italy, a positive impression was expressed with reference to the potential impact of NAS restrictions on auditors' independence, as per the following opinion:

> *[T]he structure of the rules on independence [...] has greatly improved compared to the previous one, especially as regards non-audit services.*
>
> (Regulator, Rome, 2018)

Italian Big Four auditors participating in the interviews recognise that being part of a multidisciplinary network is an advantage, because the audit team's specialists (e.g., information technology, tax, risk management) help improve audit quality:

> *Certain activities cannot be carried out on audit clients, but they can help maintaining within the network those same competencies that, on the one hand, are useful to the audit team to perform a good work and, on the other hand, may be offered to the market as far as NAS clients are concerned.*
>
> (Big Four auditor, Milan, 2018)

Both auditors and audit committee/Board of Statutory Auditors (BSA) members in Italy confirmed that higher attention is paid also to the tendering process and to how the audit mandate can prevent audit firms from accepting more lucrative NAS. It was reported on several occasions that audit services are significantly less profitable than NAS, and that some audit companies admit to avoiding tenders to have the possibility of offering to their clients a range of NAS that are more lucrative, which is what we also discovered from the UK participants:

> *If the network is already providing some significant (and profitable) activities, s/he [the auditor] might decide not to participate in the tender.*
>
> (Big Four auditor, Milan, 2018)

With the EU reform, there will be more cases where Italian auditors may decide not to take part in their client's tender if they prefer to keep carrying out more lucrative NAS activities for that client. Italian audit committee/BSA members raised strong criticism about NAS provision by audit firms, sometimes even using colourful expressions:

> *Auditors are paying high attention to the new rules. Audit partners act like a truffle dog monitoring deadlines and jobs.*
>
> (BSA member, Milan, 2019)

As a result, both UK and Italian audit firms are considering NAS provision and EU restrictions when choosing strategically their participation in the tendering process of PIEs. Perception issues are raised by regulators and standard setters in the UK; however, the key in both countries is whether actual independence is maintained. Balancing these audit independence perception issues against the need for audit firms to maintain a profitable business model, continue to adopt emerging technologies, and be conscious of shareholder concerns, as mentioned above, is not easy. In the past, it was alleged that auditors expected NAS work after finishing the auditing job, perhaps as some type of reward. Their auditor independence can also be affected by the risks of self-review. Self-review threats arise from external auditors reviewing their own work or the work done by others in their firm. It may be more difficult to evaluate without bias one's own work or that of one's audit firm than the work of someone else or of some other audit firm. Therefore, a self-review threat may arise when external auditors review judgements and decisions they or others in their audit firm have made. In sum, the provision of NAS by an incumbent auditor has remained a highly contentious issue. It is generally assumed that external auditors should know the effects of threats on an auditor's independence, and should abide by the rules of professional behaviour, and exercise suitable defensive procedures against these independence threats.

5.3.2 Impacts that are specific on smaller audit practitioners

In both the UK and Italy, there is general agreement that the NAS reforms will create more opportunities for non-Big Four auditors to sell NAS or audit services to new clients due to the restrictions that the EU reforms impose (Kend et al., 2021). Some auditors in the UK have argued that it will be up to audit committees to decide whether they wish to be more associated with the smaller practitioners, whether this is for audit services or NAS. The CMA report (2018) found that the average sales of NAS to audit clients appears to be slightly higher for the smaller firms than for the Big Four: in 2018, the average value of NAS to their audit clients was around 4% of audit fees for the smaller firms, compared with 38% for the Big Four auditors. Some argue that, with future audit tenders in mind, smaller practitioners are being considered for new NAS work, to allow for relationship building. Audit tendering considerations are impacting the allocation of NAS work based on the views of the participants in the UK.

> *I think we have the smaller firms getting more NAS work. As to whether that is because of the NAS ban and the fee cap I think is a moot point because I think it is more to do with the "How can we get to know these firms for future tenders?"*
>
> (Big Four auditor, London, 2018)

Italian auditors indicated that the NAS restrictions due to EU Audit Reforms may provide new opportunities for smaller auditors to widen their market base and profits. The services that are now prohibited from being carried out by the audit firm can be carried out by different and smaller audit companies, thereby providing an opportunity for growth for these businesses. This is consistent with the views from the UK. Two main elements were indicated by Italian auditors (both Big Four and non-Big Four) with reference to the effects of NAS restrictions for smaller practitioners.

First, in Italy, non-Big Four auditors aim at collaborating with Big Four auditors rather than competing directly. On several occasions, non-Big Four auditors admitted that they are making more and more effort to build and strengthen their relationships with Big Four auditors. In this way, they aim at becoming the main, local service provider offices of Big Four companies, who will call upon them when their clients require restricted or prohibited NAS. As a result, auditors from non-Big Four firms indicate how they continuously develop advisory services related to tax and legal support, which are the main prohibited NAS activities.

Second, in Italy, non-Big Four firms are targeting two different categories of potential clients: (1) non-listed companies or companies that opt for voluntary audits; and (2) PIEs whose auditors cannot carry out a prohibited NAS. As non-Big Four auditors indicated, smaller practitioners can find new opportunities for business in tax and legal services, which can also be more profitable and involve lower risks than audit services. Audit committee/BSA members also confirmed that they would certainly consider non-Big Four auditors for NAS, while it is more difficult to suggest the latter to PIEs because of the high standard of audit required by the market.

Likewise, in the UK we find some audit committees reluctant to consider non-Big Four auditors for PIEs:

> *I think it depends on how many companies are willing to make sure they invite non-Big Four firms to tender for their audits of large listed companies. So, I think it depends on how each audit committee pushes or is willing to have firms outside the Big Four involved.*
>
> (Non-Big Four auditor, London, 2018)

5.3.3 Stricter authorisation processes related to NAS within the audit firms

An important consideration is whether the current framework for managing NAS conflicts is sufficient to focus auditor's incentives on high-quality audits. One way to address the reality and perception of NAS-related conflicts would be to structurally separate audit and NAS. Depending on the specific implementation, this might return PIEs to greater choice among the Big Four. However, there would also likely be substantial costs and disruption to the firms, according to the CMA report (2018). In general, from the main views of UK participants in the present study on having NAS restrictions and on auditors providing NAS to their audit clients, these views are mixed. Some interview respondents indicated that the EU Audit Reforms made little change to the UK audit services market, while others mirrored the views of the CMA report (2018) and made calls for a total ban on NAS to audit clients:

> *My personal view is I would ban the non-audit services. They can sell whatever non-audit services they want to the non-audit clients, so I would ban it to audit clients.*
>
> (Professional accounting body, London, 2018)

In Italy, the participants do not convey the radical views of structurally separating audit and NAS work, as proposed in the UK. Instead, at a general level, auditors, and audit committee/BSA members in Italy, indicated that the restrictions introduced with the EU Audit Reform did not entail a radical change in the already existing practices and risk management processes; however, they underlined how the stricter and more detailed restrictions have increased the attention the audit firms pay when assessing the NAS provided to their clients:

> *I can say there has been no significant change. In fact, the only difference is that the authorisation process has now become stricter since, before the reform, it did not expressly require a favourable opinion from the audit committee/BSA.*
>
> (Big Four auditor, Verona, 2018)

At the audit firm level, in Italy auditors indicated how the authorisation process for NAS has become more strictly enforced. From the auditors' perspective, there is an increased attention regarding both the NAS content and the related fee caps, which may force the auditors to either reduce the number of working hours or reject some assignments to avoid risks. As there was already a list of incompatible NAS before the EU reform, Italian audit companies had an internal control system in place to detect activities that are restricted or prohibited and, thereby, automatically reject those that were incompatible. With the EU Audit Reform and the more detailed list of prohibited NAS, these internal control systems have been improved and strengthened. The information system stores information about all firms' clients and acts as a "sentinel" by monitoring (usually monthly) all the services that are provided to each client:

> [...] *we have an internal system where all the clients' information is stored [...] the system is called "sentinel". Every partner is a lead partner for each client and, consequently is the person responsible for giving authorisation to both Italian and foreign entities for the provision of every type of service.*
>
> (Big Four auditor, Verona, 2018)

Prior to acceptance, a proposal is to be run by the system, and a digital authorisation must be granted. The procedure has different layers of authorisation according to the type of service that is to be authorised. When a listed company and NAS are involved, the internal control procedure includes more verifications than the ones required for regular audit services or for non-listed companies. In the case of NAS for listed companies, controls are run through the audit partner, the risk manager, the technical director, and the audit manager, all of whom are to authorise the service for it to be accepted.

At the audit committee/BSA level in Italy, both auditors and audit committee/BSA members indicated an increment in the attention paid to the content and the type of additional services provided by the audit company. Indeed, NAS that are requested by a client are to be assessed and authorised by the client's audit committee/BSA as well. As audit committee/BSA members are now held responsible for NAS authorisation as part of their duties, they are demanding additional disclosure on NAS to the audit firm. A BSA member referred to situations where requests have been made to anticipate the end of the audit firm's mandate to waive the restrictions on NAS, which were assessed and analysed very carefully, with request for more information by the BSA:

> *[...] so, the company wrote to us [the BSA members] saying that it would have been the case to tender largely in advance and according to*

a certain way, but I don't even think to do that, because whether you (the auditor) provide audit services or you do not.

(BSA member, Milan, 2018)

Among the Italian regulators that participated, the overall judgement on the AC/BSA role in NAS authorisation is positive. However, the interviewees highlight that the NAS evaluation for big, multinational groups of companies is a very difficult task for AC/BSA. Thus, they are guessing whether it could be feasible for AC/BSA to adopt a sort of resolution frame as a guideline to decide on NAS and whether CONSOB, the Italian Financial Market Authority, itself could offer specific recommendations on this issue to the benefit of AC/BSA.

5.4 Summary

The EU reforms made little change to the UK audit services market; likewise, in Italy, where existing practices were already in place to deal with NAS restrictions. In the UK some participants mirrored the views of the CMA report (2018) and made calls for a total ban on NAS to audit clients, whereas in Italy such suggestions were not raised, as a certain level of confidence exists in the risk management processes and controls that are already in place related to the provision of NAS.

The CMA recommended an operational split of firms in the UK, with the regulator responsible for designing specific elements of the separation and refining it over time. The CMA proposal (2018) would initially apply to the "Big Four" firms in the UK. Regulators should consider extending elements of the operational separation principles to the non-Big Four firms. The key features of this recommendation included:

- the creation of a new board for the audit practice, which would be responsible for remuneration decisions and developing and maintaining audit quality standards.
- a requirement to produce separate financial statements that would reflect the costs of services provided by the non-audit part of the firm.
- a requirement that profits should not be shared between the audit and non-audit practice (DBEIS, 2021).

In making these recommendations, the CMA decided against an alternative proposal that would have mandated a full structural separation between audit and non-audit functions. However, the UK government around 2019 consulted on the CMA's proposals in relation to operational separation and respondents broadly agreed with the CMA's suggestion to create separate governance structures within audit firms. Respondents disagreed with specific aspects of the CMA's proposals, including its proposal to prevent profit sharing, which some stakeholders suggested would erode the multidisciplinary culture within audit firms and result in a loss of access to expert non-audit staff (DBEIS, 2021). As discussed in Chapter 4, the EU recently introduced mandatory audit firm rotation, which may result in a cyclic alteration of audit firm roles as providers of audits and NAS (Quick, 2022). We are yet to experience the perceived benefits of mandatory audit firm rotation in the EU and what that will mean for the NAS market in the medium to long term. In the UK the provision of NAS to a PIE audit client is now limited to services regarding legally required reports and audit-related services (Quick, 2022). Moreover, the Big Four audit firms must operationally separate their audit and NAS practices by 30 June 2024 (FRC, 2020c). The latter should ensure a focus on audit quality and protect auditors from influences from the NAS practice (Quick, 2022).

References

Aschauer, E., and Quick, R. (2018). Mandatory audit firm rotation and prohibition of audit firm provided tax services: Evidence from investment consultants' perceptions. *International Journal of Auditing,* 22: 131–149. https://doi.org/10.1111/ijau.12109.

Austin, A., Carpenter, T., Christ, M., and Nielson, C. (2021). The data analytics journey: Interactions among auditors, managers, regulation, and technology. *Contemporary Accounting Research*, forthcoming. https://doi.org/10.1111/1911–3846.12680.

Beardsley E., Imdieke, A., and Omer, T. (2021). The distraction effect of non-audit services on audit quality, *Journal of Accounting and Economics,* 71. https://doi.org/10.1016/j.jacceco.2020.101380.

Cameran, M., and Santoli, E. (Eds.) (2018). Il mercato della revisione contabile in Italia al 31-12-2017. SDA Bocconi - Osservatorio di Revisione. Available at: http://osservatoriorevisione.sdabocconi.it/. Accessed 27.06.2019.

Christ, M.H., Emett, S., Summers, S.L., and Wood, D. (2021). Prepare for take-off: Improving asset measurement and audit quality with drone-enabled inventory audit procedures. *Review of Accounting Studies*, forthcoming. https://doi.org/10.1007/s11142-020-09574-5

Competition & Market Authority—CMA (2018). *Statutory audit services market study.* London: National Archives.

European Commission (2017). Report on monitoring developments in the EU market for providing statutory audit services to public-interest entities pursuant to Article 27 of Regulation (EU) 537/2014.

Financial Reporting Council (2020a). The use of technology in the audit of financial statements, AQR Thematic Review, March 2020. London, UK.

Financial Reporting Council (2020b). Discussion Paper: Technological resources: Using technology to enhance audit quality, March 2020. London, UK.

Financial Reporting Council (2020c). Objectives, outcome, and regulation. London, UK.

Friedman, H., and Mahieux, L. (2021). How is the audit market affected by characteristics of the non-audit services market? *Journal of Accounting Research.* https://doi.org/10.1111/1475-679X.12347

Garcia-Blandon, J., Argiles-Bosch, J., Castillo-Merino, D., and Martinez-Blasco, M. (2017). An assessment of the provisions of regulation (EU) No 537/2014 on non-audit services and audit firm tenure: Evidence from Spain. *The International Journal of Accounting*, 52(3): 251–261. https://doi.org/10.1016/j.intacc.2017.07.003

Horton, J., Tsipouridou, M., and Wood, A. (2018). European market reaction to audit reforms. *European Accounting Review*, 27(5): 991–2013.

Houghton, K., Kend, M., and Jubb, C. (2013). The CLERP 9 audit reforms: Benefits and costs through the eyes of regulators, standard setters and audit service suppliers. *ABACUS: A Journal of Accounting, Finance and Business Studies*, 49(2): 139.

ICAEW (2022). Auditor independence approach. London, UK. Available at: https://www.icaew.com/technical/trust-and-ethics/ethics/auditor-independence/auditor-independence-approach. Accessed 31.07.22.

Kend, M., and Nguyen, L.A. (2020). Big data analytics and other emerging technologies: The impact on the Australian audit and assurance profession. *Australian Accounting Review*, 30: 269–282.

Kend, M., Leoni, G., Florio, C., and Gaia, S. (2021). *EU audit reforms: Analysing different impacts in the UK and Italy*. London: ICAEW.

Kend, M., and Nguyen, L. (2022). The emergence of audit data analytics in existing audit spaces: Findings from three technologically advanced audit and assurance service markets. *Qualitative Research in Accounting and Management*, 19(5): 540–563. https://doi.org/10.1108/QRAM-01-2021-0005

Lombardi, R., Cosentino, A., Sura, A., and Galeotti, M. (2021). The impact of the EU Directive on non-financial information: Novel features of the Italian case. *Meditari Accountancy Research*. https://doi.org/10.1108/MEDAR-06-2019-0507

Quick, R. (2022). Can prohibitions of non-audit services and an expanded auditor liability improve audit quality? *International Journal of Auditing*. https://doi.org/10.1111/ijau.12268

Ratzinger-Sakel, N.V.S., and Schönberger, M.W. (2015). Restricting non-audit services in Europe: The potential (lack of) impact of a blacklist and a fee cap on auditor independence and audit quality. *Accounting in Europe*, 12(1): 61–86.

Ruhnke, K., and Schmidt, M. (2016). Changing the institutional framework of statutory audit: Internal stakeholders' perceptions of the associated benefits and costs. *European Accounting Review*, 25(1): 59–79.

Salijeni, G., Samsonova-Taddei, A., and Turley, S. (2019). Big data and changes in audit technology: Contemplating a research agenda. *Accounting and Business Research*, 49: 95–119.

UK Government, Department for Business, Energy, and Industrial Strategy (DBEIS) (2021). Restoring trust in audit and corporate governance: Consultation on the government's proposals.

6 Audit committees

Greater powers and proposed standards

6.1 Introduction

The audit committee (AC) plays a critical role in corporate governance practices by overseeing the quality of auditing. An effective and independent AC with relevant expertise is expected to enhance approaches to auditing which contribute to improved audit quality (Sulaiman, 2017). The AC is now required to assess and monitor various aspects of the external auditors, which include the appointment and remuneration of auditors, auditor independence, and the effectiveness of the audit process, to attain high audit quality (FRC, 2018). However, Sulaiman (2017) conveys that caution should be taken in assessing the ability of ACs to discharge the expected oversight function. This chapter provides an overview of the main findings of studies that have investigated the effects of regulations on AC function and powers, with a particular focus on the EU Audit Reform (2014). It also provides a qualitative analysis of key perceptions of auditors and regulators of the key impacts of the EU Audit Directive (2014/56/EU) and Regulation (537/2014) in terms of ACs' powers.

6.2 An overview of the changes in the powers and roles of AC

The EU Audit Directive (2014/56/EU) and the EU Audit Regulation (537/2014) have strengthened the role and responsibilities of the ACs which were already set in the previous Directive 2006/43/EC. These include four monitoring responsibilities in relation to the financial reporting process, the effectiveness of the internal control and risk management system (including the internal audit, when applicable), the statutory audit of annual and consolidated accounts, and the independence of the statutory auditor (EU Audit Reforms 2014a, 2014b). They also include one recommendation about AC responsibilities which relate to the proposal for the appointment of the statutory auditor (Van der Elst, 2015). The literature on how regulatory changes have impacted on powers and effectiveness of the AC is still emerging, with limited evidence existing on the oversight role of the AC in

DOI: 10.4324/9781003262596-6

the post-governance reforms (Sulaiman, 2017) and the EU Audit Reform (2014) (Kend et al., 2021).

Most of the literature that has investigated the impact of audit regulation on ACs mostly focuses on the US (see Ghafran and O'Sullivan (2013) for a comprehensive review of these studies). This is likely to be because the US has been one of the first countries in the world to introduce audit reforms that, with the use of legislative requirements, specifically focus on ACs (Ghafran and O'Sullivan, 2013). Within Europe, several reforms related to ACs have been adopted. These were mostly of a non-legislative nature and based on a "comply or explain" approach (Collier and Zaman, 2005), until the time the establishment of ACs was made mandatory for the public interest entities (PIEs) operating in an EU Member State with the Directive 2006/43/EC (EU, 2006). Despite this, when compared with the US literature, a relative number of studies have investigated the impact of audit recommendations in Europe. Most of these studies have focused on the UK institutional setting, as the UK has been one of first countries in Europe to issue corporate governance recommendations as regards ACs. These studies have investigated the effectiveness of these recommendations mostly in terms of audit and non-audit fees and financial reporting quality, providing overall support to their effectiveness. Motivated by the introduction of new recommendations made by the Smith Committee (2003) pertaining to the structure of ACs, Zaman et al. (2011) investigated the impact of AC effectiveness, measured in terms of independence, expertise, diligence, and size, on audit and non-audit fees. Their results show a positive association between AC effectiveness and audit fees only for larger firms and a positive association between AC effectiveness and non-audit fees for all firms, and especially for the larger ones. The authors conclude that their findings provide support to the importance of the regulatory changes introduced by the Smith Committee (2003). Mangena and Pike (2005) investigated the effects of the recommendations made, in the UK, by the Cadbury Committee (1992) and the Smith Committee (2003) that ACs should review interim disclosures. This is done by empirically examining the relationship between some AC characteristics (namely, AC shareholding, AC size, and AC financial expertise) and the level of disclosure provided in the interim reports published by a sample of UK listed companies. Their findings show that the level of interim disclosure is negatively and significantly associated with AC shareholding, while positively and significantly associated with AC financial expertise. No significant relationship has been found between interim disclosure and AC size. The authors' conclusions support the recommendations made by the Cadbury Committee (1992) and the Smith Committee (2003) on the AC being involved in reviewing interim disclosure. They also suggest the inclusion of certain AC characteristics as they are paramount in enhancing their oversight roles. Similar results are found by Song and Windram (2004) who investigate the effectiveness of UK ACs in their responsibility of overseeing financial reporting quality, as set by the Smith Committee (2003). Using a sample of companies that have been subject to adverse rulings by the Financial Reporting Review Panel (FRRP), the authors show that ACs whose members are less independent, have share ownership, and have multiple directorships are less effective in overseeing the financial reporting process. Li et al. (2012) investigate the effectiveness of the recommendations made by the UK Code (FRC, 2010), the Smith Committee (2003), and the Financial Reporting Council (FRC, 2012a) in relation to AC size, AC share ownership, AC composition, and AC meetings' frequency in terms of the quality of intellectual capital (IC) disclosure. Using data from 100 UK listed firms, the authors find that IC disclosure is positively associated with AC size and frequency of meetings, and negatively associated with ACs' shareholding. No significant association was found between IC disclosure and AC independence and financial expertise. Overall, their results support the effectiveness of the UK recommendations about certain AC characteristics. Alzeban and Sawan (2015) investigate the association between AC characteristics and the perceptions of the implementation of the AC recommendations set by the FRC with the Guidance on Audit Committee and the Corporate Governance Code (FRC, 2012a, 2012b). Using data from a survey of chief internal auditors, the authors find that greater perceptions of the implementation of these recommendations are strongly related to AC independence and the presence of AC members with expertise in accounting and auditing and, to a lower extent, to the frequency of meetings between the AC and chief internal auditors. Overall, the evidence provided by the studies conducted in the UK institutional setting supports the effectiveness of the recommendations made by UK regulators aimed at promoting AC effectiveness.

Pre-EU Audit Reform (2014) studies conducted in Europe, outside the UK institutional setting, and aimed at evaluating the effectiveness of AC recommendations were rarer and less supportive of the effectiveness these recommendations, when compared with the studies conducted in the UK. Among these studies, the study of Böhm et al. (2013) is particularly relevant as it investigates how Directive 2006/43/EC (EU, 2006) has been transposed into national legislation. This Directive mandated EU PIEs to establish an AC, required them to assign AC-specific responsibilities, and required that at least one AC member be independent and have competence in accounting and/or auditing. Focusing on Belgium, France, Germany, Italy, Spain, and the Netherlands, the findings of the study show that Directive 2006/43/EC has been effectively implemented, via the issuance of corporate governance codes' recommendations. However, substantial cross-national differences in the scope of responsibilities assigned to ACs, the expertise and competences required of AC members, and their independence were found.[1] The study also explored how companies have responded to these normative changes, showing that most of the corporations studied, particularly those based in France, Germany, and Italy, provided disclosures that did not resemble the recommendations given by the respective national corporate governance codes. These results suggest that corporations question the effectiveness of the new regulation. Other studies have investigated the effectiveness of the recommendations issued in relation to the AC and its composition in terms of financial reporting quality and aspects related to the audit process. Pucheta-Martínez and De Fuentes (2007) investigate if the likelihood of receiving a qualified audit is associated with the AC existence and its characteristics, based on the recommendation stated by the Spanish Code of Corporate Governance (CEECECAS, 1998). Their findings show that AC size and independence affect the likelihood of receiving error or non-compliance qualifications, but not the likelihood of receiving audit reports containing uncertainties or scope limitations. Piot and Janin (2007) study the role of the AC in preventing the use of earnings management in France. Relying on the recommendation of the Vienot Code (Viénot, 1995, 1999) and Bouton report (Bouton, 2002), the authors' findings show that AC presence, but not its independence, curbs upward earnings management. The authors believe that independent AC members do not play a significant role as the regulation does not clearly define their responsibilities within the AC. They conclude arguing that recommendations or regulations about AC independence are likely to be ineffective if their duties and responsibilities are not clearly specified. Focusing on the Italian institutional setting, Romano and Guerrini (2012) examine the association between the presence and independence of the AC, as recommended by the Italian Code of Corporate Governance (1999, 2002), with the publication of corporate accounts that fail to comply with legal and regulatory provisions. Their findings show no significant associations, questioning the effectiveness of the AC and its independent members. Zarza Herranz et al. (2020) investigated, in a large sample of European firms based in eight different Member States, the relation between AC expertise and certain features of the audit process. The study shows that ACs with greater expertise tend to pay lower audit fees, whereas no association was found in relation to changes in the external firm audit. In their conclusions, the authors stress the importance for the EU to pay more attention to directors' expertise, by providing clearer definitions of the different competencies that AC members must possess and explaining how these competencies can be gained. Overall, the European studies conducted outside the Anglo-Saxon domain seem to be less supportive of the effectiveness of the recommendations and regulations issued in relation to the AC.

Very few research studies have been conducted to evaluate the impact of the regulations that resulted from the EU Audit Reform (2014). Drogalas et al. (2021) and Chalevas et al. (2021) investigate its impact in the Greek institutional context. Drogalas et al. (2021) examine the relationship between AC characteristics and audit and non-audit fees after the implementation of the Directive, using a sample of 126 Greek listed companies. Their findings show that AC size, AC members' expertise, and the frequency of AC meetings are positively associated with audit fees, as well as board size. Based on these results, the authors question the effectiveness of the new regulation, as they interpret the association between board size and audit fees as an indication of the Board of Directors playing a key role in supervising and compensating the auditors, whereas, in line with the requirements of the EU Audit Reform (2014), this should completely lie on the AC. The study of Chalevas et al. (2021) uses the responses provided by 138 Greek PIEs to a questionnaire on their compliance with the EU Audit Reform (2014) requirements in relation to the AC, to investigate the impact of the Directive on financial reporting quality. Their results show the PIEs analysed extensively adopted the requirements of the Directive, and that these lead to a significant enhancement of financial reporting quality. This is true particularly in relation to the requirements related to AC composition and skills, AC duty to make statutory auditors understand the business of the entity, and AC responsibilities to monitor statutory auditors' independence and the effectiveness of the PIEs' internal quality control. Van Liempd et al. (2019) focused on the Denmark setting to study the perceived usefulness of the EU Audit Reforms (2014) in relation to the joint provision of audit and non-audit services. The authors found that the role of the AC on the preapproval of non-audit services is not regarded as important in enhancing auditor independence. The authors suggest that this might be due to the respondents' lack of confidence in the competence of the AC in identifying possible independence threats.

In addition, two technical research reports have been published by the ICAEW and Deloitte with the aim of enhancing the understanding of how ACs have evolved and are functioning after the enactment of the EU Audit Reform (2014) (ICAEW, 2017, 2019). The 2017 study surveyed ACs' members in several Eastern European countries (Bulgaria, the Czech Republic, Hungary, Lithuania, Poland, Romania, and Slovenia), showing that ACs in these countries play an increasingly key role in ensuring financial reporting quality. Despite this, several challenges that require attention were noted, of which the most important were related to issues of digital and data security and the implementation of the EU Audit Reform (2014) (ICAEW, 2017). The 2019 study examines the evolution of ACs in other six EU countries (Belgium, Cyprus, Greece, Malta, the Netherlands, and Portugal) after the enactment of the EU Audit Reform (2014). This is with the aim of assessing how they respond to the technological transformation of business and society and the changes in corporate reporting and corporate governance frameworks. The findings of the report highlight an increasing demand on ACs' time and greater attention to the skills and experiences of its members. They also show that ACs are busy in dealing with the changes in corporate reporting and corporate governance frameworks, as well as with those resulting from the continuous technological transformation of businesses and society.

Limited empirical evidence exists in relation to the effectiveness of the requirements introduced by national and supranational regulations and recommendation on the ACs in Europe, and in relation to those introduced by the EU Audit Reform (2014). The few extant studies conducted in the aftermath of the latter are consistent in showing the key role that AC expertise, AC independence, and AC time commitment played in enhancing the effectiveness of the AC in monitoring the accounting and auditing processes and financial reporting quality. This emerging literature also questions the role played by the AC in supervising and compensating the external auditors, one of the new responsibilities that the EU Audit Reform (2014) has assigned to the AC. Not very much is, however, known in relation to the impacts that such reforms will make in term of other ACs' responsibilities. The following sections aim to fill this gap and contribute to the emerging literature on the AC and the EU Audit Reform (2014), by discussing the key impacts that auditors and regulators believe the Directive will make in terms of the different ACs' powers, focusing in particular on its responsibilities to select, supervise, and compensate the external auditors and to use the additional written audit report that the audit firm must provide the AC with in improving financial reporting quality.

6.3 The perceptions of the impacts of the EU Audit Reform on ACs' powers

The EU Audit Reform (2014) assigns greater powers to the ACs appointed by PIEs. Main changes refer to: (1) audit firm selection and tenure; and (2) the additional written report that the auditors provide ACs.

First, the AC is now more responsible for the audit firm selection procedure. The selection procedure is organised by the future audited company according to strict criteria that require the following: (1) an open invitation to all audit firms willing to submit proposals for statutory audit services to the company; and (2) a set of tender documents with the detailed description of the company's business and the type of statutory audit required. As a result, the tender process does not preclude the participation of minor audit firms. In addition, selection criteria, if any, shall be defined and made public in advance by the to-be-audited company. Based on the received proposals, the AC submits its own recommendation with at least two choices for the audit engagement and a duly justified preference for one of them. Finally, at the general meeting of shareholders of the audited company, the PIE makes the final decision and appoints the audit firm (which might be different from the one recommended by the AC). At all times, the AC oversees and checks whether the auditor's independence is threatened and, where necessary, implements any safeguard measures to eliminate or reduce the risks of incompatibility to an acceptable level.

Second, the AC now receives an additional written report from the audit firm. This report explains the results of the statutory audit carried out and, *inter alia*, describes the nature, frequency, and extent of communication with the AC, the auditing methodology used, and any significant deficiencies or matters in the audited entity. In turn, the AC informs the Board of Directors (or equivalent body) of the audited company about the outcome of the statutory audit and explains how the latter contributed to the integrity of the financial reporting.

6.3.1 Impacts from the new role of the AC in selecting the statutory auditor

The EU Audit Directive (2014/56/EU) and Regulation (537/2014) were designed to strengthen the role of the AC to better align the auditor's incentives with shareholders, rather than with company management. However, the evidence from the CMA report (2018) does not inspire confidence that ACs consistently prioritise quality. A UK study by Sulaiman (2017) found that the conduct of the AC in relation to audit quality involves the assessment of the contents of the reports prepared by the external auditors for the AC. Furthermore, the oversight of audit quality by the AC involves a thorough assessment of the presentation of the external auditors during the interaction and communication between the two parties. This illustrates the AC's role as an effective monitoring mechanism when overseeing the audit quality. However, Sulaiman (2017) highlights the ceremonial role of the AC in overseeing four major areas (independence, appointment, remuneration, and effectiveness of audit process), which demonstrates the limited supporting role of the AC in enhancing audit quality. AC members view their role as mediators; they commonly express an earnest desire to maintain their independence from and scepticism about corporate governance actors while accomplishing role-relevant objectives (Obermire et al., 2021). Further, research such as DeZoort and Salterio (2001) finds that AC members with financial reporting and auditing knowledge are more likely to understand auditor judgements and support the auditor in auditor-management disputes than members without such knowledge. Moreover, financially knowledgeable members are more likely to address and detect material misstatements. So, research is mixed on whether ACs play a supporting role in enhancing audit quality; thus further research is needed.

One way to re-orient the incentives on auditors to focus on providing high-quality audit based on professional scepticism and challenge would be to remove the responsibility for the audit selection processes, and for audit engagement monitoring, from companies altogether (CMA, 2018). These responsibilities could instead be undertaken by an independent body. The CMA report (2018) suggests that this would break the link between company management and audit firm appointment and reappointment – creating an environment where audit firms are better incentivised to provide quality audits. The UK participants in this study acknowledged greater responsibilities for ACs and their need to be more demanding of the external auditors when evaluating the written reports about the audit process. However, most of these changes occurred through the UK's corporate governance code, unlike in Italy where the changes that have impacted ACs came into effect later via the EU Audit Reform (2014):

> *The UK corporate governance code, so the FRC has used that to put in some of these changes, so essentially it changed the relationship and brought audit committees more back into the limelight from an audit perspective that they yield the external audit relationship. I think the audit committees would be more responsible, I think, this was quite a big change.*
>
> (Regulator, London, 2018)

In Italy, as presented in Chapter 2 of this book, according to the corporate governance model adopted by each company, the AC can be represented by the Board of Statutory Auditors (BSA). When considering Italy, reference is made to the AC/BSA. The AC/BSA role within the process of the audit firm selection entails different perceptions in Italy. In principle, the filter provided by the AC/BSA is defined as a "*common sense type of thing*" (BSA member, Milan, 2019), and the codification of the selection procedure is appreciated because it fills a lack of regulation that has generated uncertainty and inefficiency in the past in Italy. However, several criticisms were raised during the focus groups, revealing that Italian AC/BSA members are not fully convinced about the actual benefits of this more transparent selection procedure:

> *The procedure is a mess because of the required public tender that must guarantee non-discriminatory access to all audit firms.*
>
> (BSA member, Milan, 2019)
>
> *The recommendation by the AC is a farce because the AC is not totally free in its recommendation. I expect the preferred candidate will always be suggested in our ears, the management is entitled to conduct direct negotiations with interested tenderers in the course of the procedure … and in all cases the general assembly of shareholders undertakes the final decision.*
>
> (BSA member, Verona, 2019)

In this regard, Italian auditors did not say much. But they appear to look at – and appreciate – the UK experience in the selection process:

> *We have seen that in the UK the tenders for the PIEs, and so the choice of the auditor, it's done without considering the amount of fees required. This is an element (fees) that potentially may not be considered anymore by the audit committee in the auditor choice [also in Italy]. As a result, the fees become a contractual aspect between the nominated auditor and the client that needs/wants to change the auditor.*
>
> (Big Four auditor, Milan, 2018)

In particular, Italian auditors recognise that this tender process without indication of fees brings two main benefits: (1) the audit firm needs now to focus its proposal on the quality of its audit service, which is based on its knowledge of the industry, its organisational structure, and its system for audit quality review; and (2) in analysing the tenders, the AC is relieved from considering the economic offer, which is always a difficult matter when assessing professional services.

In summary, there are substantial changes as proposed by the CMA report (2018) that can be made to the current AC framework to ensure that auditor incentives are appropriately aligned towards quality. However, given the opposition participants reported from shareholders concerned about being disenfranchised in the CMA report, we perhaps need to better understand how ACs work with the statutory auditors, and this might be possible now due to their increased responsibilities. Italian AC/BSA members are not fully convinced about the benefits of the more transparent AC rules and procedures for auditor selection and appear to be more questioning of these changes than the UK participants, because these changes are more recent in Italy, as they were already in built into the UK system before the EU Audit Reform (2014) due to the corporate governance code changes made by the FRC.

6.3.2 *Impacts from the new reports to the AC*

The CMA reported in 2018 that many other stakeholders overwhelmingly opposed replacing ACs with an independent body. Thus, alternatively, if other options are to be considered where ACs are given greater powers, we need to better understand how they work together with external auditors under the current UK Governance Code and the EU Audit Reform (2014). Our findings from the UK indicate that a greater role for ACs exists currently, and that they must become more demanding of auditors yet maintain good communication with the audit partners and the audit team. These findings are consistent with prior research (such as Obermire et al., 2021) that suggests AC members are actively involved in monitoring management as well as trying to mediate and bring together multiple parties to derive effective and equitable solutions to enhance effectiveness. The UK respondents highlighted this need to maintain good communication with audit partners and their teams, and to keep them independent, but did not refer to the (internal) reports that auditors provide to the AC, as indicated by Italian participants:

> *I mean, ultimately, it comes down to the audit committee to ensure that they have sufficient choice. In theory, audit committees should be monitoring what the potential auditors are looking at doing, examining the amount of work that they're doing for entity and keeping them independent.*
>
> (Professional accounting body, London, 2018)

> *So, I think that it's important that the audit committee chair needs to be pretty much an open book with the audit partner. You hope that helps the auditor do a better job, but hopefully, it also gives confidence to that lead audit partner, that s/he really can say what s/he thinks.*
>
> (Audit committee chair, London, 2018)

In Italy, this report from the audit team was heavily emphasised and referred to by participants. As a first insight, both auditors and AC/BSA members in Italy underlined that there has always been cooperation between the audit team and the AC/BSA and that such cooperation implies the systematic arrangement of meetings. However, the additional report to AC/BSA is highly appreciated as a formalised step that was previously missing, because the exchange of opinions on audit matters often remained informal while a clean opinion was issued by the auditor.

Because of the EU Audit Reform (2014), the AC/BSA now receives a specific report that requires the auditors to "*talk about what they have seen and done*" (BSA member, Milan, 2019). In turn, the AC/BSA is called upon to deliver to the Board of Directors this additional report, accompanied with the observations of the AC/BSA itself. Because of the additional report and observations by the AC/BSA, the so-called management letter that the audit firm used to issue to the benefit of the Board of Directors has disappeared in practice. This new role of the AC/BSA has been widely appreciated because the AC/BSA is entitled to access the firm's accounting structures, documents, and processes, and is now in a condition to act as a (competent and experienced) filter between the audit firm and the Board of Directors:

> *Personally, I have welcomed the reform because it provides an important signal, the one-off identifying, within the PIE, a body able to interface between the company's structures and the audit firm, a body that could not have been the Board of Directors. ...The AC has now become a central step of verification of the activity performance by the audit firm. It also can go ahead in its activity with sufficient authority.*
>
> (BSA member, Verona, 2019)

> *My judgment is overall positive. The true change is that before the EU Reform, things were separated and not very transparent, while after the EU Reform, information circulates, and everybody is called to formalize any concern that previously remained into the fold of the audit report.*
>
> (BSA member, Verona, 2019)

Besides appreciation for the new role attribute to the AC/BSA, some criticism also arose during the focus groups with AC/BSA members in Italy and even with the participants from the Italian regulator. A first aspect refers to the new and higher risks that the AC/BSA is now exposed to because of these new requirements, with AC/BSA members recognising what follows:

> *These several steps will enable the auditors' activity if the auditor recognizes their potentials, while they downgrade the same activity when the auditor acts like a mere executor of procedures, the Board of Statutory Auditors serves as a paper-pusher without making remarks, and maybe even the Board of Directors overlooks the report. But if everyone does his job seriously, then the new requirements are welcome.*
>
> (BSA member, Milan, 2019)

A second area for criticism regards the overlapping between the extended audit report, the additional report written by the audit firm for the AC/BSA, and the observations to be reported by the AC/BSA:

> *Basically, observations from the AC/BSA reiterate critical issues, i.e., KAMs, already underlined by the statutory auditors. In my experience, ACs are not going much further. It is a mechanism for discharging accountability from both sides.*
>
> (BSA member, Verona, 2019)

In this regard, one of the Italian regulators provides some thoughts on the current situation and future perspectives on the relationship between AC/BSA and the audit firms:

> *Further improvements in the whole process will be possible when the AC/BSA will realize what it is concretely called to do. Then, it will act a very important role for the evaluation of auditor's independence, not only to the purpose of auditor's selection but also in progress, during the mandate execution. [...] Further, an increased awareness on the new AC/BSA role is necessary also on the auditor's side because we perceive that when the AC/BSA goes deeper into irregularities or other issues, the auditor shows a certain intolerance and the information exchange on his side is not yet immediate, nor optimal.*
>
> (Regulator, Rome, 2019)

Finally, a third critical area is indicated in the gap between the deeper knowledge, competence, and responsibility that is now required of AC/BSA members and compensation to the latter:

> *Overall considered, the AC plays an important role, but companies often want to save right on the compensation of those who operate controls.*
>
> (BSA member, Milan, 2019)

6.4 Summary

It has been suggested by prior research (Zabri et al., 2016) that knowledgeable ACs help enhance the company's performance; therefore, good characteristics of ACs are associated with good company performance. An effective AC is expected to emphasise optimisation of shareholders' wealth and prevent managers' maximisation of their personal interests (Zabri et al., 2016). This chapter reports that in the UK the impacts of the changed role of ACs are not perceived as a relevant change, as opposed to in Italy, where participants indicate that the EU Audit Reform (2014) has increased the power in the hands of AC/BSA members in the choice of the auditor. There is also indication in Italy of a general appreciation of the exclusion of economic considerations in the auditor selection process as a further regulatory intervention. Similar perceptions are gathered regarding the new reports to the ACs. Indeed, in the UK there is reference to a continuous effort of the auditors in maintaining good communication flow with the ACs. In Italy, such an indication is provided as well, but with even more detail regarding the appreciation of the increased disclosure enabled by the new reports to the ACs/BSAs. However, some criticism was raised regarding the related increase in responsibilities that came with such higher amounts of disclosure. This is consistent with the findings of some prior studies (such as Obermire et al., 2021) that suggest AC members simply serve as a risk mitigation tool, more so than adding value to the governance process.

Note

1 In particular, the study shows that Spain and the Netherlands indicated a broader scope of responsibilities to be assigned to the AC, while France, Italy, and Germany assigned the AC fewer ones. In term of competences, the six countries transposed the EU Reforms (2014) requirement by defining financial expertise differently, and only Spain and France extended this requirement to all the members of the AC. However, in terms of AC independence, all countries gave stringent recommendations than those set by the EU Audit Reform (2014). Belgium, French, and Italy recommended all AC members to be non-executive and most of them independent, whereas the Netherlands recommended that only one AC member may not be independent.

References

Alzeban, A., and Sawan, N. (2015). The impact of audit committee characteristics on the implementation of internal audit recommendations. *Journal of International Accounting, Auditing and Taxation,* 24: 61–71. https://doi.org/10.1016/j.intaccaudtax.2015.02.005

Böhm, F., Bollen, L.H., and Hassink, H.F. (2013). Spotlight on the design of European audit committees: A comparative descriptive study. *International Journal of Auditing,* 17(2): 138–161. https://doi.org/10.1111/j.1099-1123.2012.00461.x

Bouton, D. (2002). *Pour un meilleur gouvernement des entreprises coteées – Rapport du groupe de travail présidé par Daniel Bouton.* Mouvement des Entreprises de France (MEDEF) & Association Française des Entreprises Privées (AFEP-AGREF), September, Paris.

Cadbury Committee (1992). *Report of the Committee on the financial aspects of corporate governance.* London: Gee.

CEECECAS (Comité Especial para el Estudio de un Código Etico de los Consejos de Administración de las Sociedades) (1998). *El Gobierno de las Sociedades Cotizadas, Comité Olivencia.* Madrid: CEECECAS.

Chalevas, C., Giannopoulos, P., Koutoupis, A., and Samara, A. (2021). Evaluating the role and effectiveness of the audit committee on the quality of financial reporting: Evidence from Greek PIEs. *International Journal of Banking, Accounting and Finance,* 12(4): 368–388. https://doi.org/10.1504/IJBAAF.2021.10041386

Collier, P., and Zaman, M. (2005). Convergence in European corporate governance: The audit committee concept. *Corporate Governance: An International Review,* 13(6): 753–768. https://doi.org/10.1111/j.1467-8683.2005.00468.x

Competition and Market Authority – CMA (2018). *Statutory audit services market study.* London: National Archives.

DeZoort, F., and S. Salterio, S. (2001). The effects of corporate governance experience and financial reporting and audit knowledge on audit committee members' judgments. *Auditing: A Journal of Practice and Theory,* 20 (September): 31–47.

Drogalas, G., Nerantzidis, M., Mitskinis, D., and Tampakoudis, I. (2021). The relationship between audit fees and audit committee characteristics: Evidence from the Athens Stock Exchange. *International Journal of Disclosure and Governance,* 18(1): 24–41. https://doi.org/10.1057/s41310-020-00088-9

European Union (2006). Directive 2006/43/EC of the European Parliament and of the Council of 17 May 2006 on statutory audits of annual accounts and consolidated accounts. *Official Journal of the European Union,* 49(L 157): 87–107.

European Union (EU) (2014a). Directive 2006/43/EC of the European Parliament and of the Council of 17 May 2006 on statutory audits of annual accounts and consolidated accounts. Available at: https://eur-lex.europa.eu/legal-content/EN/TXT/HTML/?uri=CELEX:32014L0056&from=EN. Accessed 15.03.19.

European Union (EU) (2014b). Regulation (EU) No 537/2014 of the European parliament and of the council of 16 April 2014 on specific requirements regarding statutory audit of public-interest entities and repealing Commission Decision 2005/909/EC. Available at: http://eur-lex.europa.eu/legal-content/EN/TXT/PDF/?uri=CELEX:32014R0537&from=EN. Accessed 15.03.19.

FRC (2010). The UK Corporate Governance Code, June. Available at: https://www.frc.org.uk/getattachment/31631a7a-bc5c-4e7b-bc3a-972b7f17d5e2/UK-Corp-Gov-Code-June-2010.pdf

FRC (2012a). *Guidance on audit committees.* London: FRC. Available at: https://www.frc.org.uk/getattachment/9ac07916-ea56-4027-864a-11ef9bfa24e4/Guidance-on-Audit-Committees-(September-2012).pdf

FRC (2012b). *The UK corporate governance code.* London: FRC. Available at: https://www.frc.org.uk/getattachment/e322c20a-1181-4ac8-a3d3-1fcfbcea7914/UK-Corporate-Governance-Code-(September-2012).pdf

FRC (2018). The UK corporate governance code. Available at: https://www.frc.org.uk/getattachment/88bd8c45-50ea-4841-95b0-d2f4f48069a2/2018-UK-Corporate-Governance-Code-FINAL.pdf. (Assessed 26.12.2021).

Ghafran, C., and O'Sullivan, N. (2013). The governance role of audit committees: Reviewing a decade of evidence. *International Journal of Management Reviews*, 15(4): 381–407. https://doi.org/10.1111/j.1468-2370.2012.00347.x

Herranz, C.Z, Lopez-Iturriaga, F. and Reguera-Alvarado, N. (2020). Audit committee expertise in large European firms. *Managerial Auditing Journal*, 35(9): 1313–1341. https://doi.org/10.1108/MAJ-11-2019-2478

ICAEW (2017). *Making a difference. Audit committees in central and Eastern Europe*. London: ICAEW.

ICAEW (2019). *Facing changes. Audit committees in Europe*. London: ICAEW.

Italian Code of Corporate Governance (1999). *Codice di Autodisciplina*. Milan: Borsaitaliana.

Italian Code of Corporate Governance (2002). *Codice di Autodisciplina*. Milan: Borsaitaliana.

Kend, M., Leoni, G., C. Florio, C., and S. Gaia, S. (2021). *EU audit reforms: Analysing different impacts in the UK and Italy*. London: ICAEW.

Li, J., Mangena, M., and Pike, R. (2012). The effect of audit committee characteristics on intellectual capital disclosure. *The British Accounting Review*, 44(2): 98–110.

Mangena, M., and Pike, R., (2005). The effect of audit committee shareholding, financial expertise and size on interim financial disclosures. *Accounting and Business Research*, 35(4): 327–349. https://doi.org/10.1080/00014788.2005.9729998

Obermire, K., J. Cohen, J., and K. Zehms, K. (2021). Audit committee members' professional identities: Evidence from the field. *Accounting, Organizations and Society*, 93, (in press), https://doi.org/10.1016/j.aos.2021.101242.

Piot, C., and Janin, R. (2007). External auditors, audit committees and earnings management in France. *European Accounting Review*, 16(2): 429–454. https://doi.org/10.1080/09638180701391030

Pucheta-Martínez, M.C., and De Fuentes, C. (2007). The impact of audit committee characteristics on the enhancement of the quality of financial reporting: An empirical study in the Spanish context. *Corporate Governance: An International Review*, 15(6): 1394–1412. https://doi.org/10.1111/j.1467-8683.2007.00653.x

Romano, G. and Guerrini, A. (2012). Corporate governance and accounting enforcement actions in Italy. *Managerial Auditing Journal*, 27(7): 622–638. https://doi.org/10.1108/02686901211246778

Smith, Report (2003, January). *Audit Committees—Combined code of guidance (the Smith report)*. London: Financial Reporting Council.

Song, J., and Windram, B. (2004). Benchmarking audit committee effectiveness in financial reporting. *International Journal of Auditing*, 8(3): 195–205. https://doi.org/10.1111/j.1099-1123.2004.00090.x

Sulaiman, N. A. (2017). Oversight of audit quality in the UK: Iinsights into audit committee Conduct. *Meditari Accountancy Research*, 25(3): 351–367. https://doi.org/10.1108/

Van der Elst, C., (2015). European legislative framework for audit committees. *The European Company Law*, 12: 26.

Van Liempd, D., Quick, R., and Warming-Rasmussen, B. (2019). Auditor-provided nonaudit services: Post-EU-regulation evidence from Denmark. *International Journal of Auditing*, 23(1): 1–19. https://doi.org/10.1111/ijau.12131

Viénot, M. (1995, July). *Le conseil d'administration des sociétés cotés*. Paris: Association Française des Entreprises Privées (AFEP) & Conseil National du Patronat Français (CNPF).

Viénot, M. (1999, July). *Rapport du comité sur le gouvernement d'entreprise présidé par M. Marc Viénot*. Paris: Association Française des Entreprises Privées (AFEP) & Mouvement des Entreprises de France (MEDEF).

Zabri, S. M., K. Ahmad, K., and K. K. Wah, K.K. (2016). Corporate governance practices and firm performance: Evidence from Top 100 public listed companies in Malaysia. *Procedia Economics and Finance*, 35: 287–296. https://doi.org/10.1016/S2212-5671(16)00036-8

Zaman, M., Hudaib, M., and Haniffa, R. (2011). Corporate governance quality, audit fees and non-audit services fees. *Journal of Business Finance & Accounting*, 38(1–2): 165–197. https://doi.org/10.1111/j.1468-5957.2010.02224.x

7 The future of audit

Impacts of new technologies

7.1 Introduction

In Chapter 7 we introduce how emerging technologies have created what can be described as a digital revolution in audit, and how this "revolution" is perceived to have impacted the audit business model. There is scant prior knowledge about how interactions among audit clients, auditors, regulation, and technology affect the diffusion (i.e., intertwined development, use, and spread) of technology across the audit reporting environment (Austin et al., 2021). The revolution of technology is rapidly tackling various prospects in the field; however, there remains uncertainty about future outcomes (Kruskopf et al., 2019). Specifically, for auditing, the quality and timeliness value of implementing computerised tools into conventional procedures are substantial. Key technologies driving this ongoing technological change include artificial intelligence (AI) that encompasses machine learning (ML), deep learning (DL), data analytics, robotic process automation (RPA), and distributed ledger technology (DLT). To understand how these emerging technologies have created a digital revolution in audit, and how this "revolution" is perceived to have impacted the audit business model, we surveyed a sample of 85 European auditors in 2022, as an extension to the original fieldwork completed in 2018 and 2019, when 23 auditors were interviewed. Due to the accelerated pace of development of these technologies, questions are posed on how auditors are dealing with change. Questions asked are regarding the potential advantages and challenges posed by data analytics, ML, blockchain, and AI, and how these technologies can improve (or not) the auditors' practices. Indeed, in such a context, data quality, privacy, and the expectations of market regulators and financial statement users may inhibit the widespread use of such technologies in the audit sector. This chapter tries to shed some light on the potential advantages and challenges of these new technologies referring to both the more recent audit literature and the insights conveyed by a sample of 85 surveyed auditors and the more in-depth interviews from 2018/2019 within the sub-set of participants (23 auditors out of 50 total interviews).

DOI: 10.4324/9781003262596-7

7.2 The digital revolution

The continuous evolution of digital technologies, especially in the past two decades, has brought the introduction of innovative technologies in businesses, service providers, hospitals, as well as governmental and non-governmental organisations (EY, 2016; KPMG, 2016). Further, the digital culture has already shown to be capable of profoundly changing any decision-making processes with new technologies replacing humans in the production and certification of knowledge, and the making of decisions (Quattrone, 2016). In every field, organisation, or profession, digital technologies have allowed for new and disruptive ways of collecting, storing, elaborating, and analysing data (Arnaboldi et al., 2017). The digital revolution is disrupting and changing the traditional approach to several professions, including the audit profession (Kokina and Davenport, 2017). Thus, it is no surprise that the impact of the digital revolution on audit is gaining increasing attention in the accounting and auditing literature (Lamboglia et al., 2021), especially to establish the implications for the profession of the diffusion of different digital technologies.

When the internet was introduced in the 1990s – also known as the Web 1.0 period – users were passive, as they only searched for information or exchanged simple messages and emails. Between the 2000s and the 2010s, we shifted to the Web 2.0 period with increasing interactions among internet users and the so-called co-production of information and web content supported by the possibility to share through advanced devices and social media like Facebook, Twitter, YouTube, and the like. From the 2010s we entered the Web 3.0 period characterised by even more interactions and exchanges of data and contents made possible by the "cloud." In this period, the sharing is not limited to data and information but extends to the technologies that become "distributed" among different users/contributors and are partially autonomous thanks to algorithms and AI (Choudhury, 2014; Pencarelli, 2020). We are fully immersed in the Web 3.0 era and assist in the surge of technologies such as ML, AI, and the Internet of Things. All these new technologies are aimed at facilitating humans in the understanding and analysis of data, thereby allowing them to become more productive and quicker. Among many others, audit professionals have been dealing with understanding, analysing, and auditing a large amount of accounting data, traditionally without the facilitation of any advanced digital technology. While the new digital technologies may support the data analysis in the audit activities, it is still unclear how the audit professionals will adapt, get trained, and use these tools in their traditional activities. There is a growing body of accounting literature that aims at unpacking the different impacts of the introduction of new technologies for auditing and auditors (Schmitz and Leoni, 2019). The evidence is still varied and limited, although everyone agrees that the audit profession will not disappear but will need to adapt or change.

Numerous analytical tools have long been applied in the auditing profession. Audit data analytics (ADA) involves the extraction of data using fields within the basic data structure, extrapolating trends, metrics, and correlations to make decisions. With the advent of advanced analytics using ML and DL algorithms, ADA tools can make predictions, identify anomalies, and discover trends in the form of diagnostic, predictive, and prescriptive analytics. The benefits of using ADA tools on audits include: (i) the ability to test an entire dataset, (ii) granular insights into the client's business processes, (iii) robust fraud detection techniques, and (iv) the ability of auditors to concentrate on providing advisory services by outsourcing repetitive tasks to machines. Further benefits of ADA tools include the analysis and testing of entire datasets, rather than selected samples, data visualisation, and interrogation options, all directly contributing to enhanced audit quality. However, these technologies also have their disadvantages, and these should be noted. For instance, ML technology is poised to provide more opportunities for auditors to focus on the bigger picture, but it is important to note the limitations: the size, scope, and quality of inputs of the ML algorithms. Due to the potential flaws in the data output, ML algorithms require good quality data that are sufficiently large, and all users should understand the nature of inputs, data, outputs, and potential biases.

7.3 Audit and technology: a review of the initial literature

The relationship between the new digital technologies and the audit profession has attracted growing academic attention in the past few years (Lamboglia et al., 2021), providing several insights from different perspectives. In their bibliometric analysis of this topic, Lamboglia et al. (2021) provide an overview of the more recent literature on the topic. We use it as a reference to provide a summary of the literature on audit and new digital technologies, to be contrasted with the insights gathered from the survey and the in-depth interviews with European auditors.

Initial research on the topic is strongly linked to information technology (IT) research. The first studies consider the introduction of electronic audits (Bedard et al., 2003) and the factors affecting the implementation of such technologies in audits (Curtis and Payne, 2008). They are mainly on IT research, with a limited focus on the content and issues of audit procedures. A similar approach is also recognised in another topic area, regarding the implementation of a continuous audit or continuous monitoring (Kuhn and Sutton, 2010) as a tool for real-time assurance and improvement of audit efficiency (Chan and Vasarhelyi, 2018). Continuous monitoring is found to be adopted because there is an expectation of audit performance improvement (Gonzalez et al., 2012), and is generally used in internal audit practices (Lombardi et al., 2015). Still with a major focus on the "IT side," other works have focused on the construction of computer-assisted audit tools and software to identify the pros and cons of these tools in improving audit activities (Dowling and Leech, 2007; Kuhn and Sutton, 2010; Van der Aalst et al., 2011; Geerts et al., 2013; Singh et al., 2014; Hardy and Laslett, 2015). Beyond the technical aspects of the tools, these studies offer initial evidence on the challenges of introducing new technologies and training auditors, while respecting their goals and work habits.

There is anecdotal evidence from audit partners which indicates that some leading audit firms have started to adopt new technological tools and techniques in practice; however, Gepp et al. (2018) in their study reveal a consensus that some emerging technologies are somewhat underutilised in auditing thus far. Auditors need to balance what the new technologies bring with the appropriate use of data, and then evaluate potential unintended consequences or audit risks (Kend and Nguyen, 2020). Thus, as these new technologies in audit become more routine in audit practice, professional auditing standards will need to evolve to address the challenges that these technologies currently present in the audit profession. The UK regulator, the Financial Reporting Council (FRC, 2020a), stated that emerging technologies, such as ML and predictive analysis, although largely at a research stage, present further opportunities to improve audit quality but also raise challenges for both audit firms and market regulators in terms of compliance with audit standards. Due to the absence of technology being incorporated into the current auditing standards (Byrnes et al., 2014), Whitehouse (2014) suggests the need for having regulators react faster to technological advancements, such as ADA. Researchers such as Christ et al. (2021) interviewed national-level partners and audit standard setters and highlighted impediments to adopting these technologies, including audit firm concerns about being first movers combined with the inability of audit standard setters to guide at a pace that matches the pace of technological development.

Another group of research reflects on the impacts of digital technologies implementation on the audit profession, rather than on the technicalities of such technologies. Concerning the use of ADA, which can include ML, DL, big data analytics (BDA), RPA, blockchain or DLT, up to AI, several studies have investigated how these technologies – together or separately – may affect or change the audit profession, procedures, and quality, using two different approaches. On the one hand, a group of studies provides insights via literature reviews and viewpoints, to highlight the main issues under discussion within the literature and provide some insights for future research, especially because their implementations are still in their infancy (Gepp et al., 2018). Initial research has discussed how BDA may improve the efficiency and effectiveness of financial statement audits (Cao et al., 2019) and auditor judgements (Brown-Liburd et al., 2015). With regard to the use of AI, ML, and DL, other reflective works state that such tools have the potential to deeply change the audit process and the range of audit services that auditors can offer (Kokina and Davenport, 2017; Raschke et al., 2018). Similarly, within the realm of blockchain technology (BT), which has been depicted as a game changer in the audit profession, initial studies have reviewed academic and professional literature to consider the main advantages and challenges of BT introduction in the audit profession. The most cited works have considered how the audit professionals will not be replaced by the new technologies and will gain more time to be allocated to more relevant and subjective audit services (Schmitz and Leoni, 2019) and discussed the potential implications, limits, and improvements that the BT may bring to the auditors' activities (Bonsón and Bednárová, 2019; Kend and Nguyen, 2020; Dyball and Seethamraju, 2021a, 2021b; Lombardi et al., 2022).

On the other hand, other studies provide insights on the above topic by sharing the professionals' and stakeholders' perceptions on the matter because the use of large sample statistical analyses or case studies is limited, or due to the lack of data on technology implementation. This literature speaks directly with the content of the present chapter and will be discussed in contrast with the findings from our survey and interviews. Among the most important studies, Tiberius and Hirth (2019) have found that auditors' opinions in Germany are varied and uncertain, but all point to the maintenance of a role for the auditors, who will be supported by the new digital technologies of BDA. Further, Kend and Nguyen (2020) looked at the perceptions of Australian auditors and audit clients and found that they expect that BDA, AI, and RPA will take auditors away from manual and standardised tasks and give them more time for complex audit judgements. Dyball and Seethamraju (2021a, 2021b) found that auditors perceive their blockchain clients as riskier, due to the lack of consensus and professional experience on accounting standards in blockchain applications, thereby making the audit activity more difficult and uncertain. Similarly, Gauthier and Brender (2022) found that, according to auditors, the present audit standards are required to keep pace with new technologies and to adapt if audit quality is to be maintained robust and relevant. The Kend and Nguyen (2022) study examined the interaction of key stakeholders (auditors, non-Big Four auditors, audit regulators, and audit committee members) with ADA technologies from a developed country context (Australia, New Zealand, and the UK). Advancements are revitalising the technologies not only of external auditors and their firms but also of their audit clients (Kend and Nguyen, 2022). Although the audit model is changing, external auditors are reported to be reluctant to fully engage with new audit technologies. Kend and Nguyen (2022) raise calls for regulators to be more up to speed with these new technological changes, as audit standards need to be amended accordingly. While the International Auditing and Assurance Standards Board (IAASB) deliberates, both clients and auditors need to lobby for specific ADA regulations. Developments in technology have affected how entities operate and process information, such as the increased use of AI, robotics, cloud computing, digital currencies, and payment platforms (IAASB, 2020). Simultaneously, developments in technology have affected how external audits are performed, for example, the use of ADA, ML, and AI (IAASB, 2020). Many external auditors have made substantial investments in automated tools and techniques to replace or supplement manual audit procedures. Changes brought about by factors such as big data and social media have further affected the sources and volume of information available to entities and external auditors (IAASB, 2020). The FRC (UK) (2020b) stated that a key challenge for the audit profession is to ensure that auditing standards remain fit for purpose, setting objectives and requirements for auditors which are designed to ensure consistent delivery of high-quality audits, whilst allowing for innovation and deployment of increasingly sophisticated technological resources.

As a result, evidence is still limited on the perceived impacts of new technologies in audit and oftentimes confined to a single country. The present chapter will contribute to advancing the knowledge in this area by providing the opinions of European auditors on a variety of aspects related to new technologies, such as the degree of use of new technologies in audit, the different uses by Big Four and non-Big Four, as well as the client willingness to engage in new technologies to facilitate the auditors' job.

7.4 Research methodology

To collect the perceptions of European auditors on the development of new technologies within the audit profession, the research has entailed two phases. In the first phase, various rounds of interviews with 23 Italian and UK auditors were performed in 2017, 2018, and 2019 on diverse audit issues as part of a larger research project, from which initial insights on the impacts of new technologies and some concerns on the future of the profession had arisen. Such insights were used in the second phase to construct a mix of 19 closed and open-ended questions for a survey to be submitted in early 2022 to European auditors and former auditors to gather deeper insights on new technologies in audit and the future of the profession. The survey was filled by 85 respondents, but we only obtained full responses from 49 respondents that completed the survey. Potential survey respondents were contacted directly following a snow-balling approach or via a general invitation to complete the survey through the authors' LinkedIn accounts and Twitter pages. The 19 survey questions include 8 biographic questions, 7 closed questions based on the Likert scale, and 4 open-ended questions where respondents could provide long answers in textual form (Appendix). The questions cover both impacts of new technologies in audit and the future of the audit profession. In this chapter, the insights on the impacts of new technology from both the preliminary interviews and the 2022 survey are considered.

The analysis of the survey data entailed the analysis of the distributions of the Likert scale responses for the closed questions, whilst the written texts of the open-ended questions were analysed via a thematic analysis to identify new themes or integrate those from the preliminary interviews. Thematic analysis is a method that allows for the systematic identification and organisation of themes through the identification of patterns of meaning within texts (Braun and Clarke, 2012). After familiarising themselves with the texts, the authors separately proceeded with the manual codification of all texts to identify codes via an iterative process. The codes were then discussed among the authors and grouped into themes (Braun and Clarke, 2012).

The survey respondents were 49 in total, from Italy (78%), the UK (9%), Spain (2%), Germany (2%), and the Netherlands (2%). Most respondents are male (74%). More than half of the respondents are between 25 and 50 of age, with 23% between 25 and 30, and 31% between 41 and 50 (Table 7.1). Almost half the respondents have more than ten years of experience in the audit profession (55%), while the 39% have less than ten years of experience in the field. About 40% of the respondents are audit partners, while the rest occupy junior (14%) or less senior (18%) positions. In terms of previous education, around 26% hold a bachelor's degree, about 47% hold a master's degree, and only a small group hold a PhD (13%) or an MBA degree (6%).

7.5 Digital revolution and its impact on the audit profession: perceptions from the field

The survey results provide various insights on the digital revolution within the audit sector on the level of expertise of the surveyed European auditors around digital technologies and their perceptions concerning the use of technologies by audit firms and clients. Further, the 2022 survey reports insights on the main challenges and opportunities technologies are expected to present for the audit profession, which integrate and extend the ones collected with the preliminary interviews from 2018/2019.

7.5.1 Level of expertise of auditors and perceived diffusion of emerging technologies among auditors and clients

The 2022 survey highlights the level of knowledge and expertise that European auditors have with new digital technologies. Many of the respondents admit to having intermediate expertise in digital technologies (49%) or being a novice (20%), while those with advanced preparation are a minority (18%). While it seems that auditors have experience with some technologies, they appear to have very limited experience with others (Figure 7.1). Indeed, the respondents affirm knowing business analytics (25%), cloud computing (18%), text or data mining (16%), data visualisation tools (15%), and AI (10%). However, only a few respondents claim to have experience with natural language processing (4%), DL (4%), robotics (3%), or Python (3%). While respondents seem to have almost no experience or little experience concerning ML (1%), blockchain (1%), or drones (0%).

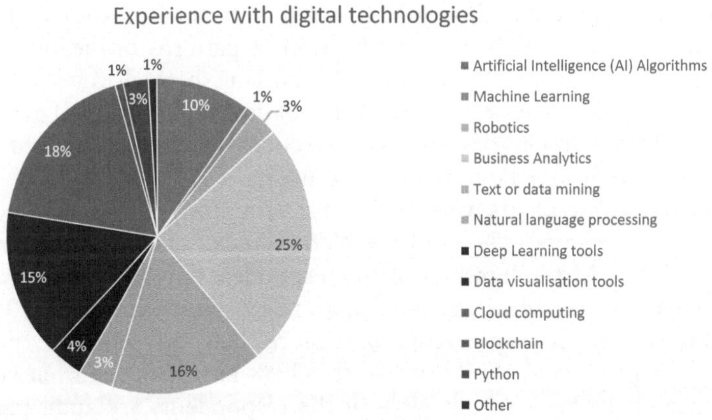

Figure 7.1 Distribution of auditors' experience by type of digital technology.

The growing expertise of auditors and their interest in the new emerging audit technologies is sustained by the idea that such technological advancements, new audit tools, and techniques are a valuable addition to the audit profession and can enhance the audit process, which is agreed upon by a large majority of the respondents (94%). According to the respondents, there are positive impacts in the introduction of new technologies, as they are perceived to have created new forms of audit evidence (89% of respondents) and have allowed conducting reports on the forecast of estimates, going concerns, and fraud detection in a more cost-effective manner (60% of respondents). This is also supported in the following excerpts when auditors state:

> *Technologies can speed up the standard process for audit evidence and support the human Partner to manage correctly the external opinion.*
>
> (Survey – Auditor 11)

> *They [the technologies] allow to make the audit procedure more efficient and to reduce the probability of errors.*
>
> (Survey – Auditor 23)

> *Information systems should help extend sampling, carry out specific analyses on anomalies identified by artificial intelligence programs and therefore should endure a higher level of reliance on the procedures performed.*
>
> (Survey – Auditor 74)

However, despite the general optimism concerning the positive impacts of new technologies, the respondents (70%) highlight that some technologies are underutilised in audits, and this is confirmed by how the knowledge of certain technologies is distributed among the respondents (Figure 7.1). According to some respondents (38%), this underutilisation may be due to the reluctance shown by some practitioners, while according to others (36%) the audit firms have not yet found solutions to the high costs to be incurred to introduce advanced technologies in their day-to-day activities (Kend and Nguyen, 2022), especially if they are smaller firms:

> *Older and smaller auditors cannot make this effort, because of age, because of lack of willingness, because of lack of financial resources.*
>
> (Survey – Auditor 29)

> *Not all the auditors (especially the smaller ones) are capable of investing in the emerging technologies.*
>
> (Survey – Auditor 39)

However, the opinions regarding the impacts of new technologies (and their costs) on smaller and larger firms are quite varied among the respondents, attesting to different experiences and situations within the industry. According to the respondents, the larger audit firms are those facing the bigger pressures to continuously keep pace with technological advancements (76%), while smaller firms are indicated as less subject to pressure, as only 21% of respondents recognised high pressure for smaller firms as well. Indeed, 67% of respondents agree that larger firms are more exposed to competition than smaller firms, thereby being forced to stay on top of technological changes in the industry. However, some further comments from the respondents provide insights into the underutilisation of new digital technologies by larger firms, as well. Indeed, larger firms are said not to be "championing" the new technologies because of a lack of knowledge of their full potential, rather than a lack of resources. A respondent underlined the following:

> *Auditors, especially the Big4, ignore the huge amount of data they are "sitting on". Indeed, without violating any privacy regulation, they miss out on the great potential of aggregated data from business analytics. They are not aggregating the huge amount of financial data they have access to, thereby failing to use such macro-data to provide better advisory services to their clients when it comes to price variance of raw materials, industry trends, procurement, and supply strategies. For instance, by aggregating data of many companies throughout the years, it is possible to estimate the price change of raw materials and advise their clients on how to improve their procurement strategies or whether to enter a certain business.*
>
> (Survey – Auditor 47)

Another important aspect that may drive the diffusion of new digital technologies in the audit profession is also the ability and willingness of audit clients and their response to technological change. Indeed, the preliminary interviews had already indicated the need for auditors to upgrade their technical skills to support clients that are expected to become more and more technological:

> *Companies will certainly adopt the latest technological tools. Maybe dematerialising the cash flow and, accordingly, auditing will have to keep abreast of all these technological innovations to meet the stakeholders' requirements in an even more accurate way.*
>
> (Big Four auditor, Verona, 2018)

This suggests that one of the factors driving the technological change of auditors is the client-side demand for it, which is confirmed by 60% of the survey respondents. However, technological advancement cannot be one-sided, but audit clients may need to implement technological changes to their accounting systems as well. Many of the respondents to the survey (53%) confirm that the implementation of digital technologies by audit clients may facilitate the performance of financial audits and improve the relationship between auditors and clients. However, it is conveyed that audit clients tend to be not ready for new technologies or even reluctant to pay for more advanced technological audit services (Kend and Nguyen, 2022) or specific technological support by the auditors:

> *A lot of clients are not open and ready for new technologies.*
>
> (Survey – Auditor 10)

Further, half of the respondents (53%) underline that clients question whether they should pay for such services, thereby creating another reason for the underutilisation of new advanced technologies by auditors who may lack the financial support needed to introduce advanced digital auditing systems.

As a result, there is a generally positive perception of the changes that new digital technologies have introduced or may bring to the audit profession, although there is still a lot to do in this realm to bring both larger and smaller firms up to speed with the potentials of these technologies, as well as the audit clients. Opinions are quite varied, suggesting that the change is still in the making and the road is not fully traced. For instance, it is not certain that the divide between smaller and larger firms will be accentuated by the new technologies, but it is expected that large investments will be needed to fully exploit the advantages of new technologies. Further, when it comes to audit clients, while their technological advancement is deemed useful for the audit procedures, it comes with a cost that not all clients are willing to incur, thereby suggesting that there is still variance in the implementation of advanced technologies also by audit clients.

7.5.2 *The role of regulators facing the introduction of new technologies in audit*

Another relevant insight from our research is the role of regulators facing the advent of digital technologies in the audit sector. As the auditing practice will change with the introduction of digital technologies, regulators must consider such changes as well and at a faster pace than in the past. Indeed, it normally takes much more time to revise audit regulations than to develop technical changes in the profession (Kend and Nguyen, 2022). While digital technologies evolve and enter the profession, rules must coevolve to remain relevant. However, if auditing standards are not updated accordingly, the technological change in audit may slow down. Regulators must learn the new technology, become comfortable with it, and respond by changing the audit standards where necessary. Initial concerns regarding the slowness of regulatory updates had been raised already in our preliminary interviews, where auditors underlined that existing auditing standards still refer to audit sampling, whilst these should be revised in line with the new technologies that are entering the profession:

> *At the moment, these IT tools still contrast sharply with audit principles, and it is still hard to make a connection between Big Data-related tools and auditing principles. In fact, on the one hand, audit principles will require some updates, and on the other hand, this process is irreversible.*
>
> (Big Four auditor, Verona, 2018)

The subsequent survey from 2022 has indicated that regulatory changes are perceived as too delayed concerning the pace of technological change, as 53% of respondents underline for regulators to be more up to speed with the technological changes in the audit profession, whilst only 10% of respondents think that regulators are keeping the pace. In addition, only 30% of respondents perceived real support from the International Standards of Auditing (ISA) with the diffusion and adoption of emerging technologies in the audit sector. Consequently, it is not surprising that a third of the respondents believe that auditors should lobby to pressure the regulators to make the same changes and keep pace with technological changes in the profession (Kend and Nguyen, 2022). A comment from the respondents summarises the current regulatory situation:

> *More and more become evident that the industry is running faster than the regulators: unless the rule setter updates the standards considering new technologies, audit procedures and evidence, the profession will continue to run behind.*
>
> (Survey – Auditor 81)

As a result, the interviews highlighted a need for regulators and standard setters to keep up to speed with the new technological changes in the audit industry, to better support audit processes, and to reduce the barriers to new digital technologies in audit.

7.5.3 Perceived challenges and opportunities of emerging technologies in audit

The research has also shed light on various challenges and opportunities that new technologies present for the audit profession according to the auditors. While the preliminary interviews provide evidence of some challenges and opportunities, the subsequent survey from 2022 has provided a more complete picture. In this section, we share an overview of the main challenges and opportunities resulting from the analysis of both the interviews and the open-ended questions of the 2022 survey.

Auditors agree that the digital revolution will be a challenge for the profession, because not only does it require developing a set of new technical skills but it will also force a change in the traditional auditors' mindset and approach to the job. On the one hand, auditors shall learn new sophisticated data analysis skills and continuously keep pace with technological innovations:

> *It will be challenging but we'll leave the sampling testing approach and move towards more sophisticated data analysis based on database queries, etc.*
>
> (Big Four auditor, Verona, 2018)

> *High-technological change brings real challenges which could make the audit and the audit product different. And in turn, there's a real challenge of the audit product and its relevance.*
>
> (Non-Big Four auditor, London, 2018)

> *The main challenge that the arrival of technology in the audit profession offers is to be able to keep up, to be able to bear the costs of the new technology to obtain the benefits, but also to integrate the technology into the pool of skills and competencies.*
>
> (Survey – Auditor 29)

On the other hand, there is also the need to make a shift in their traditional approach to the job, as various respondents underline. In particular, the industry may need to open to new professional figures and engage with them:

> *Compliance and IT fraud risks need to be assessed more carefully. Procedures must include the presence of IT specialists.*
>
> (Survey – Auditor 74)

> *Practitioners will need to become more confident in technical problem solving and change their mentality.*
>
> (Survey – Auditor 79)

However, once the technology becomes the new normal, auditors indicate that another challenge is related to the need to keep cultivating the "human factor" in the profession, which cannot be replaced entirely by technology:

> *The optimist in me says that the disruption of the profession is going through as it becomes increasingly a technology business and less of a people business.*
>
> (Big Four auditor, London, 2018)

> [...] *I can see more dangers than opportunities in the future of our profession since digitalising both audit and quality control processes will diminish the perception of the auditor.*
>
> (Big Four auditor, Verona, 2018)

> *To have more data and information available, at a lower cost and nearly in real-time is a good thing but human judgment in my opinion will still be the key aspect for many years to come.*
>
> (Survey – Auditor 72)

> *The risk is that technology will be preferred to the detriment of the relational and human skills of the work, which remain extremely important.*
>
> (Survey – Auditor 29)

Finally, another important challenge that the audit profession may face with the advancement of technologies is the increasing costs of the tools that may not be shared by the clients. We found that the automation of certain activities is perceived to bring the reduction of the auditors' working hours, which is the base to calculate their fees, thereby reducing the audit fees.

> *It is clear that the IT tools – if used properly – can help us to increase the quality of the work done: in fact, thanks to them we can work fewer hours and, at the same time, provide a better outcome. The real problem is that our professional fees have been always calculated on an hourly basis, while, at this moment, the network or even single national companies are making significant investments.*
>
> (Big Four auditor, Milan, 2018)

Similarly, some survey respondents also point to the higher costs of the initial investments that may slow down the implementation of technologies and increase the concentration in the market.

> *Not all the auditors (especially the smaller ones) are capable of investing in emerging technologies.*
>
> (Survey – Auditor 39)

> *The risk is more concentration in the market and the disappearance of small competitors.*
>
> (Survey – Auditor 29)

In brief, three are the main challenges of new technologies in audit as perceived by the auditors. First and foremost, auditors point to the double challenge to develop technical skills and change the traditional audit mindset. Second, it is understood that even in the presence of technology professional judgement and human factors are still – if not even more – relevant. Finally, it is said that costs may create an obstacle to the diffusion of new technologies, especially at the expense of smaller auditors that may disappear in the process.

Of course, while challenges are inevitable in a changing environment, the participants also show enthusiasm about the digital revolution, as they indicate several opportunities that may arise with technological advancement in the profession. First, the automation of basic audit activities is depicted also as an opportunity for the auditors to reduce the time spent on repetitive tasks (Kend and Nguyen, 2020). This in fact will free more working hours to be allocated to tasks that cannot be performed by machines and require professional judgement.

> *Technologies can speed up the standard process for audit evidence and support the human partner to manage correctly the external opinion.*
>
> (Survey – Auditor 11)

> *Technology can be a tool to reduce costs by speeding up work and improving customer relations, and in my opinion, it can also attract smarter and more motivated employees.*
>
> (Survey – Auditor 29)

Further, the use of ADA may also enlarge the pool of data the auditors can analyse and audit. Indeed, participants see audit technology as an opportunity to overcome the sampling approach, being able to check 100% of the company's data (Kend and Nguyen, 2020). Going beyond the sampling approach and analysing the entire population of data is also said to minimise errors and subjectivity:

> *Our profession is regulated by auditing principles, and we have always taken a sampling approach. Thanks to technological advancement, we will be probably able to adopt a different method. [...] in the auditing field, the sampling approach will be gradually replaced by more sophisticated data analysis techniques as paper archives by databases.*
>
> (Big Four auditor, Verona, 2018)

> *New technologies will allow for stronger audit evidence, better risk identification and more effective and efficient ways to audit.*
>
> (Survey – Auditor 1)

> *They allow to make the audit procedure more efficient and to reduce the probability of errors.*
>
> (Survey – Auditor 23)

> *Emerging technologies let us analyze the complete population of data.*
>
> (Survey – Auditor 38)

> *New technologies may increase the reliability of the audit procedures and therefore bring on an acceptable audit risk.*
>
> (Survey – Auditor 11)

As a result, there are two main perceived opportunities for the implementation of new technologies. First, auditors can reduce the time dedicated to standardised and repetitive tasks and allocate it to more relevant and professional tasks, where professional judgement is required (Kend and Nguyen, 2020). Second, it is largely supported that the technologies will allow auditors to analyse the full population of corporate data, thereby overcoming the weaknesses of sample-based audits, reducing the probability of errors, and, most importantly, reducing audit risk.

7.6 Summary

The above investigation presents several insights regarding the relationship between auditors and new technologies. First, it offers an overview of the level of knowledge and expertise among European auditors as well as the approach that auditors and audit clients have to new digital technologies. The results highlight that technological advancement is still in the making and opinions are varied among external auditors, especially regarding the willingness of auditors and clients to implement new technologies. The results also suggest that the industry is well-aware of the inevitable advent of new technologies in the profession but there are no signs of resistance, rather curiosity and enthusiasm. Regulation and its slower pace are perceived as risky for technological advancement in the audit profession, but it is not considered a reason for falling behind.

The investigation also identifies various threats and opportunities around high-level technological change. There are three main challenges of new technologies in audit as perceived by the auditors. First and foremost, auditors point to the double challenge to develop technical skills and change the traditional audit mindset. Second, it is understood that even in the presence of technology professional judgement and human factors are still – if not even more – relevant. Finally, it is said that costs may create an obstacle to the diffusion of new technologies, especially at the expense of smaller auditors that may disappear in the process. However, there are two great opportunities envisaged by the participants involved in our research. First, external auditors can reduce the time dedicated to standardised and repetitive tasks and allocate it to more relevant and professional tasks, where professional judgement is required. This may also attract smarter and more ambitious practitioners to the audit profession. Second, it is largely supported that the technologies will allow auditors to analyse the full population of corporate data, thereby overcoming the weaknesses of sample-based audits, reducing the probability of errors, and, most importantly, reducing the audit risk.

References

Arnaboldi, M., Busco, C., and Cuganesan, S. (2017). Accounting, accountability, social media, and big data: Revolution or hype? *Accounting, Auditing & Accountability Journal,* 30(4): 762–776. https://doi.org/10.1108/AAAJ-03-2017-2880

Austin, A., Carpenter, T., Christ, M., and Nielson, C. (2021). The data analytics journey: Interactions among auditors, managers, regulation, and technology. *Contemporary Accounting Research,* 38(3), 1888–1924. https://doi.org/10.1111/1911-3846.12680

Bedard, J.C., Jackson, C., Ettredge, M.L., and Johnstone, K.M. (2003). The effect of training on auditors' acceptance of an electronic work system. *International Journal of Accounting Information Systems,* 4(4): 227–250.

Bonsón, E., and Bednárová, M. (2019), Blockchain and its implications for accounting and auditing. *Meditari Accountancy Research,* 27(5): 725–740. https://doi.org/10.1108/MEDAR-11-2018-0406

Braun, V., and Clarke, V. (2012). *Thematic analysis.* American Psychological Association.

Brown-Liburd, H., Issa, H., and Lombardi, D. (2015). Behavioral implications of big data's impact on audit judgment and decision making and future research directions. *Accounting Horizons,* 29(2): 451–468. https://doi.org/10.2308/acch-51023

Byrnes, P., Criste, T., Stewart, T., and Vasarhelyi, M. (2014). *Reimagining auditing in a wired world.* AICPA White Paper, 11.

Cao, S., Cong, L.W., and Yang, B. (2019, June). *Auditing and blockchains: Audit pricing, misstatements, and regulation.* Working paper.

Chan, D.Y., and Vasarhelyi, M.A. (2018). Innovation and practice of continuous auditing. In Chan, D.Y., Chiu, V., and Vasarhelyi, M.A. (Eds.), *Continuous auditing (Rutgers studies in accounting analytics)* (pp. 271–283). Bingley: Emerald Publishing Limited. https://doi.org/10.1108/978-1-78743-413-420181013

Choudhury, N. (2014). World wide web and its journey from web 1.0 to web 4.0. *International Journal of Computer Science and Information Technologies,* 5(6): 8096–8100.

Christ, M.H., Emett, S., Summers, S.L., and Wood, D. (2021). Prepare for takeoff: Improving asset measurement and audit quality with drone-enabled inventory audit procedures. *Review of Accounting Studies,* 26, 1323–1343. https://doi.org/10.1007/s11142-020-09574-5

Curtis, M. B., and Payne, E. A. (2008). An examination of contextual factors and individual characteristics affecting technology implementation decisions in auditing. *International Journal of Accounting Information Systems*, 9(2): 104–121. https://doi.org/10.1016/j.accinf.2007.10.002

Dowling, C., and Leech, S. (2007). Audit support systems and decision aids: Current practice and opportunities for future research. *International Journal of Accounting Information Systems*, 8(2): 92–116.

Dyball, M.C., and Seethamraju, R. (2021a). The impact of client use of blockchain technology on audit risk and audit approach—An exploratory study. *International Journal of Auditing*, 25: 602– 615. https://doi.org/10.1111/ijau.12238

Dyball, M.C., and Seethamraju, R. (2021b). Client use of blockchain technology: Exploring its (potential) impact on financial statement audits of Australian accounting firms. *Accounting, Auditing & Accountability Journal*. https://doi.org/10.1108/AAAJ-07-2020-4681

EY (2016). *Big data and analytics* [Online]. Accessed 21 May 2022.

FRC (2020a). The use of technology in the audit of financial statements. AQR Thematic Review, March 2020.

FRC (2020b). Discussion Paper: Technological resources: Using technology to enhance audit quality, March 2020.

Gauthier, M.P., and Brender, N. (2021). How do the current auditing standards fit the emergent use of blockchain? *Managerial Auditing Journal*, 36(3): 365–385. https://doi.org/10.1108/MAJ-12-2019-2513

Geerts, G.L., Graham, L.E., Mauldin, E.G., McCarthy, W.E., and Richardson, V.J. (2013). Integrating information technology into accounting research and practice. *Accounting Horizons*, 27(4): 815–840.

Gepp, A., Linnenluecke, M.K., O'Neill, T.J., and Smith, T. (2018). Big data techniques in auditing research and practice: Current trends and future opportunities. *Journal of Accounting Literature*, 40: 102–115.

Gonzalez, G.C., Sharma, P.N., and Galletta, D. (2012). Factors influencing the planned adoption of continuous monitoring technology. *Journal of Information Systems*, 26(2): 53–69.

Hardy, C.A., and Laslett, G. (2015). Continuous auditing and monitoring in practice: Lessons from Metcash's business assurance group. *Journal of Information Systems*, 29(2): 183–194.

IAASB (2020). Project update: Revision of ISA 500, Audit Evidence. September.

Kend, M., and Nguyen, L.A. (2020). Big data analytics and other emerging technologies: The impact on the Australian audit and assurance profession. *Australian Accounting Review*, 30: 269–282.

Kend, M., and Nguyen, L.A. (2022). The emergence of audit data analytics in existing audit spaces: Findings from three technologically advanced audit and assurance service markets. *Qualitative Research in Accounting and Management*, 19(5): 540–563. https://doi.org/10.1108/QRAM-01-2021-0005

Kokina, J., and Davenport, T.H. (2017). The emergence of artificial intelligence: How automation is changing auditing. *Journal of Emerging Technologies in Accounting*, 14(1): 115–122. https://doi.org/10.2308/jeta-51730

KPMG (2016). *Analytics* [Online]. KPMG LLP. Accessed 20 May 2022.

Kruskopf, S., Lobbas, C., Meinander, H., Söderling, K., and Martikainen, M. (2019). Digital accounting: Opportunities, threats, and the human factor. *ACRN Oxford Journal of Finance and Risk Perspectives: Special Issue Digital Accounting*, 8: 1–15.

Kuhn Jr, J.R., and Sutton, S.G. (2010). Continuous auditing in ERP system environments: The current state and future directions. *Journal of Information Systems*, 24(1): 91–112.

Lamboglia, R., Lavorato, D., Scornavacca, E., and Za, S. (2021). Exploring the relationship between audit and technology. A bibliometric analysis. *Meditari Accountancy Research,* 29(5): 1233–1260. https://doi.org/10.1108/MEDAR-03-2020-0836

Lombardi, D. R., Bloch, R., and Vasarhelyi, M.A. (2015). The current state and future of the audit profession. *Current Issues in Auditing,* 9(1): P10–P16. https://doi.org/10.2308/ciia-50988

Lombardi, R., de Villiers, C., Moscariello, N., and Pizzo, M. (2022). The disruption of blockchain in auditing – A systematic literature review and an agenda for future research. *Accounting, Auditing & Accountability Journal,* 35(7): 1534–1565. https://doi.org/10.1108/AAAJ-10-2020-4992

Pencarelli, T. (2020). The digital revolution in the travel and tourism industry. *Information Technology Tourism,* 22, 455–476. https://doi.org/10.1007/s40558-019-00160-3

Quattrone, P. (2016). Management accounting goes digital: Will the move make it wiser? *Management Accounting Research,* 31: 118–122.

Raschke, R.L., Saiewitz, A., Kachroo, P., and Lennard, J.B. (2018). AI-enhanced audit inquiry: A research note. *Journal of Emerging Technologies in Accounting,* 15(2): 111–116.

Schmitz, J., and Leoni, G. (2019). Accounting and auditing at the time of blockchain technology: A research agenda. *Australian Accounting Review*, 29(2): 331–342.

Singh, K., Best, P.J., Bojilov, M., and Blunt, C. (2014). Continuous auditing and continuous monitoring in ERP environments: Case studies of application implementations. *Journal of Information Systems,* 28(1): 287–310.

Tiberius, V., and Hirth, S. (2019). Impacts of digitization on auditing: A Delphi study for Germany. *Journal of International Accounting, Auditing and Taxation*, 37: 100288.

Van der Aalst, W., Van Hee, K., Van der Werf, J.M., Kumar, A., and Verdonk, M. (2011). Conceptual model for online auditing. *Decision Support Systems,* 50(3): 636–647.

Whitehouse, T. (2014). Auditing in the era of big data. *Compliance Week,* 11: 28–67.

Appendix

Background data

What is your age group? *
Please choose **only one** of the following:

- 25–30
- 31–40
- 41–50
- over 50
- less than 25

Country of workplace: *
Please choose **only one** of the following:

- Austria
- Belgium
- Bulgaria
- Croatia
- Cyprus
- Czech Republic
- Denmark
- Estonia
- Finland
- France
- Germany
- Greece
- Hungary
- Ireland
- Italy
- Latvia
- Lithuania
- Luxembourg
- Malta

- Netherlands
- Poland
- Portugal
- Romania
- Slovakia
- Slovenia
- Spain
- Sweden
- UK
- Other

What is your highest level of education? *
Please choose **only one** of the following:

- Bachelor degree
- Master degree
- PhD
- MBA or similar
- Other

How many years of experience do you have in this field? *
Please choose **only one** of the following:

- Less than 10 years
- 11–20 years
- 21–30 years
- Over 30 years

Please identify your job title *
What is your job position? *
Please choose **only one** of the following:

- Junior
- Senior
- Manager
- Senior Manager
- Director
- Partner
- Other

Your gender *
Please choose **only one** of the following:

- Male
- Female
- Prefer not to say

Do you currently work, or have you previously worked in audit? *
Please choose **only one** of the following:

- Yes
- No

Participants' technological expertise in audit

What is your level of expertise in using technology in audits? *
Please choose **only one** of the following:

- Advanced
- Intermediate
- Novice
- No experience

Can you name the advanced technologies you are using in audits? *
Please write your answer here:
Which of the following technologies or tools do you have experience in? *
Please choose **all** that apply:

- Artificial intelligence (AI) algorithms
- Machine learning
- Robotics
- Business analytics
- Text or data mining
- Natural language processing
- Deep learning tools
- Data visualisation tools
- Cloud computing
- Using drones
- Blockchain
- Python
- Other:

New technologies in the audit profession

For all the following statements, please choose your level of agreement/disagreement with each statement (Strongly disagree; Disagree; Neutral; Agree; Strongly agree; Not applicable/prefer not to answer):

- Technological advancements, new audit tools, and techniques are a valuable addition to the audit profession.
- Advanced emerging technologies have enhanced our audit processes.
- Some emerging technologies are somewhat underutilised in auditing.
- Auditors are reluctant to use emerging techniques.

- Smaller practitioners in audit are investing in advanced audit technologies.
- The larger audit firms face the pressures to continuously keep pace with advancements in technology.
- The smaller audit firms face the pressures to continuously keep pace with advancements in technology.
- The level of competition between the larger auditors has driven the new technological demands.
- Audit firms have not yet found solutions to costing technological advancements used in external auditing.
- The demand for IT experts is increasing within the audit profession.
- Advanced technologies have generated new forms of audit evidence.
- Emerging technologies in audit allow external auditors to conduct reports on forecasts of estimates, going concern, and fraud detection in a more cost-effective manner.
- Technological advancements, new audit tools, and techniques are a valuable addition to the audit profession.
- Advanced emerging technologies have enhanced our audit processes.
- Some emerging technologies are somewhat underutilised in auditing.
- Auditors are reluctant to use emerging techniques.
- Smaller practitioners in audit are investing in advanced audit technologies.
- The larger audit firms face the pressures to continuously keep pace with advancements in technology.
- The smaller audit firms face the pressures to continuously keep pace with advancements in technology.
- The level of competition between the larger auditors has driven the new technological demands.
- Audit firms have not yet found solutions to costing technological advancements used in external auditing.
- The demand for IT experts is increasing within the audit profession.
- Advanced technologies have generated new forms of audit evidence.
- Emerging technologies in audit allow external auditors to conduct reports on forecasts of estimates, going concern, and fraud detection in a more cost-effective manner.

Regulation of new technologies in audit

For all the following statements, please choose your level of agreement/disagreement with each statement (Strongly disagree; Disagree; Neutral; Agree; Strongly agree; Not applicable/prefer not to answer):

- Regulators need to be more up to speed with these new technological changes.
- International Standards of Auditing (ISA) supports the adoption of emerging technologies in audit.
- International Standards of Auditing (ISA) supports the diffusion of emerging technologies in audit.

- Auditors need to lobby for specific audit data analytics regulation.
- Regulators need to be more up to speed with these new technological changes.
- Auditors need to lobby for specific audit data analytics regulation.

Audit clients and new technologies

For all the following statements, please choose your level of agreement/disagreement with each statement (Strongly disagree; Disagree; Neutral; Agree; Strongly agree; Not applicable/prefer not to answer):

- Audit clients are implementing new technologies that can facilitate the audits.
- Audit clients are willing to pay for the advanced technology provided and used by their external auditor.
- Audit clients question whether they should pay for such additional services new technologies may offer.
- One of the factors that impacts the progress of integrating advanced technology in the external audit includes client-side demands.
- Emerging technologies in audit enhance the relationships in a positive way between auditors and audit clients.
- Audit clients are implementing new technologies that can facilitate the audits.
- Audit clients are willing to pay for the advanced technology provided and used by their external auditor.
- Audit clients question whether they should pay for such additional services new technologies may offer.
- One of the factors that impacts the progress of integrating advanced technology in the external audit include client-side demands.
- Emerging technologies in audit enhance the relationships in a positive way between auditors and audit clients.

Attractiveness of the audit profession

- Young auditors leave the audit profession because (complete the sentence):
- Young auditors choose the audit profession because (complete the sentence):

For all the following statements, please choose your level of agreement/disagreement with each statement (Strongly disagree; Disagree; Neutral; Agree; Strongly agree; Not applicable/prefer not to answer):

- The audit profession attracts the best and brightest young auditors.
- Audit lacks the intellectual challenge needed to keep bright, high-achieving young auditors.

- Data analysis skills are becoming more and more relevant for the audit profession.
- The background and skills of young (entry-level) auditors are up to speed with new technologies available in audit.
- The audit profession attracts the best and brightest young auditors.
- Audit lacks the intellectual challenge needed to keep bright, high-achieving young auditors.
- Data analysis skills are becoming more and more relevant for the audit profession.
- The background and skills of young (entry-level) auditors are up to speed with new technologies available in audit.

Challenges and opportunities of emerging technologies in audits

- Provide your view on what are the main challenges/audit risks that emerging technologies present for the auditing profession.
- Provide your view on what are the main opportunities/advantages that emerging technologies present for the auditing profession.

8 The new paths of statutory audits in Europe

Meeting public expectations and other future challenges

8.1 Introduction

This final chapter conveys a general overview of the perceptions provided by European auditors during our research project[1] when asked about the future of the audit profession and what lies ahead for experienced and new practitioners within the next five years. Coerced by new audit regulations, within a profession that inevitably has unstable boundaries, professional external auditors are trying new ways to deliver the audit service traditionally demanded by society (Humphrey and Moizer, 1990; Samiolo, 2012). The perpetual state of change that has vibrated through external auditing has crossed boundaries that vary in time and space. This constant scrutiny and change via regulatory interventions (and government policies) has led to staff retention problems particularly at the graduate level but has also created problems by forcing changes or problems with audit methodologies and cost absorption. The main areas of hope and concern for auditors are presented in this chapter. From the problematic audit expectations gap; to the risks of more regulatory interventions, especially after Brexit; from the progressive concentration of the audit industry at the expense of the smaller firms; to the attractiveness of the auditor's job, this chapter offers insightful perspectives of European auditors. They share their views also on the future of the audit profession. Although the ones presented are the views and perceptions of auditors, the various points raised provide food for thought for audit practitioners, audit and accounting regulators, policymakers, and investors. Over the decades, auditors have faced many challenges and persistent regulatory scrutiny. For instance, Albitar et al. (2021) suggest that the effects of the Coronavirus disease of 2019 (COVID-19) pandemic will be the toughest challenge for external auditors and their clients since the 2007–2008 Global Financial Crisis (GFC). If we, for instance, take the latest global pandemic crisis, the environment in which audit judgements are made has changed substantially during the COVID-19 pandemic, and likely post-pandemic (Humphreys and Trotman, 2022). At this stage, there is little academic research that has investigated how external auditors have responded to the COVID-19 pandemic and the associated audit risks that this crisis has created for

DOI: 10.4324/9781003262596-8

their audit clients. Although beyond the scope of this book we signal that the pandemic will have long-lasting implications for the audit profession in terms of changes to audit practices, such as remote auditing and greater reliance on the emerging technology discussed under Chapter 7.

8.2 Narrowing the audit expectations gap: finding a framework for auditing in the EU

Participants involved in the interviews and survey responded to further prompting related to the future of audit in the European Union (EU), and often identified the "audit expectations gap" as an important matter of concern for the future. The concept of an audit expectations gap suggests that the society's view of the external auditors' role is different from how external auditors themselves view their true role to be (Koh and Woo, 1998; Kend et al., 2021). For instance, the Brydon Review (2019) identified fraud and external auditors' related responsibilities as the most complex and misunderstood of all the topics covered by the review and the UK government in response has since proposed a package of measures, including greater clarity regarding the respective roles of directors and external auditors, to restore public confidence in the external auditors' work (Department for Business, Energy, and Industrial Strategy, 2021). Further, there is the audit expectations-performance gap, which is defined as the gap between society's expectations of external auditors and external auditors' perceived performance (Porter, 1993). Researchers are concerned with investigating the factors contributing to the audit expectations gap and proposing solutions to help narrow the gap (De Martinis and Burrowes, 1996; Kend et al., 2021).

Basically, summarising the views expressed by these participants: governments and regulators alike express the need to find an audit system that falls into an intelligent framework of oversight, along with an overall regulatory framework for financial reporting that meets public expectations. Meeting people's perceptions of what an audit should be and delivering this to them is the "real challenge," according to several of the auditors interviewed. They emphasise that maintaining confidence in the audit system is a challenge, which is not assisted by governments that use auditors as scapegoats. This seems to be even more problematic because of the presence of too many regulators throughout the EU, which adds too many layers of complexity to achieve the desired level of communication and cooperation amongst EU Member States, as summarised in the following views:

> *The audit system that we have is fundamentally incapable of delivering to the public expectations of audit. The Government's response is always a bit more of the same and find a scapegoat of some description. They try and maintain confidence in the system that is fundamentally incapable of meeting public expectations.*
>
> (Big Four auditor, London, 2018)

> *Things need to be looked at on a much more holistic basis and in a much more intelligent basis, and whether that means fewer regulators or whether that means more effective communication and collaboration between the regulators [...].*
>
> (Big Four auditor, London, 2018)

> *My problem with the regulatory framework over the last whatever years is that it has just been additive rather than being an intelligent oversight of, "How does it fit into an overall framework of regulation?"*
>
> (Big Four auditor, Edinburgh, 2018)

In Italy, the problem of the audit expectations gap, which is an important aspect for the future development of the profession, was raised as well. On the one hand, Italian regulators maintain that the future of auditing depends on the awareness about the role of public interest that the auditors shall increasingly assume, which goes far beyond commercial aspects. On the other hand, according to Italian auditors, the issue of the audit expectations gap sits on the relationship between the controller (audit firm) and the controlled (the client), especially because the controlled is paying the controller to perform the audit. In this regard, Italian practitioners believe that there should be provisions and plans in the future to overcome such limitations in the audit profession, thereby contributing to reducing the audit expectations gap. Related to another matter, non-Big Four auditors compare their experience in performing mandatory and voluntary audit services, suggesting that the latter often represents an example of fruitful cooperation, given that in this situation the same subject pays for and benefits from the service. However, the issue about who should pay for auditing is far from being solved. According to the prevailing viewpoint of interviewed auditors, regulators should consider designing auditing systems where independence is guaranteed by a separation between the audited company and the subject who pays.

Still on the framework for auditing that may meet public expectations, Italian auditors hope that the role of statutory auditing in the market will be clarified soon:

> *Every time a new topic arises [like a recent money laundering case in a foreign subsidiary of a local bank], one of the big questions is: "Must or can the auditor intervene? Or should have the auditors intervened in that specific situation?" The answer usually is: "You should have done it because you were there looking into the financial report". However, the answers could be different. On our side the aim to always prove the work done exists and is a priority.*
>
> (Big Four auditor, Milan, 2018)

Finally, Italian auditors underline that they expect a periodic review by the Commissione Nazionale per le Società e la Borsa (CONSOB), the national independent authority that regulates the Italian capital market. CONSOB runs inspections regarding how its recommendations have been followed and to the application of the International Standards on Quality Control (Italy) that have been issued together with the International Standards of Auditing (ISA) Italy. However, Italian Big Four auditors maintain that inspections performed by CONSOB shall be improved in different aspects, and will be timely, quick, and less invasive:

> *There is a strong unbalance in the two roles [CONSOB and audit firm), in that the regulator is still very bossy when it runs its inspections: it almost puts on halt the auditor's activities, and it takes too much time to respond. [...] The asymmetry especially comes from the fact that the auditor is required to produce documentation and replies to CONSOB in 5 working days, whilst the regulator takes up to 180 days to prepare an answer and possibly provide assessments. Inspections on the quality control systems of auditors start at a certain date but provide a final report only after one year and a half up to two years. This is not manageable. Many of the recommendation arrive so late that they are useless because the auditor has already acted resulting in changes that go even beyond what CONSOB had recommended. This is at least something that needs refinements. CONSOB should do more practical and timely inspections.*
>
> (Big Four auditor, Milan, 2018)

Further issues related to regulatory interventions are discussed under the next section. However, Italian auditors do not complain about the regulator's inspections *per se*, but about their capability to provide a strategic direction to the audit process. Indeed, timelier and more practical inspections are considered helpful for improving the audit process and, in turn audit quality, as explained by this Big Four auditor:

> *Let's say that being subject to the inspection but receiving CONSOB's final report (judgment) after a long while, is at risk of disqualify the entire final report.*
>
> (Big Four auditor, Milan, 2018)

The expectations gap between auditors, regulators, and users of financial statements has long been written about; however, with corporate collapses such as Carillion in the UK, the EU regulators have once again questioned whether the whole framework of auditing oversight needs to be revisited. In the UK, action has been taken with the Kingman Review (2018) recommending enhanced monitoring of the six largest audit firms in the UK, and a new independent statutory regulator to replace the Financial Reporting Council (FRC) in late 2019. In Italy, comments about the future of the audit profession focus on finding a framework for auditing in the EU that may meet public expectations, with specific reference to the issue of who shall pay for mandatory audit services, the role of auditing in the market, and the inspections performed by regulators. With many Member States in Europe having different reforms and reviews over the years, the challenge for the EU is finding an overall regulatory framework for financial reporting that meets public expectations related to the role of auditing.

8.3 Dealing with further regulatory interventions

The audit profession has been frequently subject to regulatory reforms, especially in the last five years, and the technological changes ahead will inevitably foster further regulatory interventions. Audit standards are to be revised if new digital and data analytics tools will enter the practice, especially when sampling and audit procedures are concerned. On the one hand, participants consider fundamental that regulators keep the pace with technological innovations in the profession. On the other hand, this will mean further regulatory interventions and necessary adaptation and change in the audit practices.

The interviews and the 2022 survey have identified different concerns in different contexts about the regulators' increasing demands to the audit professionals. Indeed, in the UK the main concern of auditors is a continuous increment of the scrutiny from the government and other public reviews over the audit profession. Concern surrounds the possibility of significant structural change to the audit markets because of "headlines" and political pressures for a "shake up" of the industry. They foresee the role of the audit being questioned but emphasise that somewhere during this process we need to revisit audit quality as well. The role of the FRC in the UK has come under severe scrutiny. The new independent statutory regulator, the Audit, Reporting and Governance Authority (ARGA), will replace the FRC eventually, and is expected to be fully implemented in 2023. The new regulator will be accountable to Parliament with a new mandate, powers, and leadership. It will have an "overarching duty to promote the interests of consumers of financial information, not the producers" (Sir John Kingman Review, p. 9). The Kingman Review also recommends that the new Audit Firm Monitoring Approach (AFMA), which involves enhanced monitoring of the six largest audit firms, should not be carried out on a voluntary basis, but instead that the regulator should be given statutory power to carry out this work. Thus, from 2023 the audit profession in the UK will be under further scrutiny. The present study's semi-structured interviews in the UK were conducted before the Competition and Markets Authority's (CMA) report (CMA, 2018) was released and Kingman Review completed. They indicate that the government needs to be seen to be responding, and the CMA will have to respond due to various public pressures:

> *Regulatory interference! There's going to be some sort of shake-up because the government always needs to do something very visible to show that they've done something. It doesn't matter what the consequences are so as long as it will be in the headlines to say they've done something.*
>
> (Big Four auditor, London, 2018)

Another concern around regulatory intervention is pointed out by some Italian auditors, who lamented the increasing demands by regulators, especially at an international level, for audit on non-financial information included in the annual report and other assurance services (e.g., the quality of bank assets under management, anti-money laundering, assurance over the integrated or corporate social responsibility report). Such a demand is forcing auditors to learn how to perform audits whose focus is totally different from the traditional audit on the financial statement, which is perceived to be very important to the purpose of an internal analysis of the client's activity:

> *We are following a path that will lead us to sustainability reports. Consequently, in addition to the [audit of] financial statements we are used to draw up, there will be many other documents and more complicated reports, like sustainability reports.*
>
> (Big Four auditor, Verona, 2018)

Finally, another concern raised by European auditors regards the further regulatory interventions that will be needed to regulate the technological changes that have progressively been introduced in the performance of financial statement audits. For instance, the replacement of the traditional "human" sampling with automated data analysis of the population will require an update of the audit standards. While these interventions are considered necessary to embed various technological innovations into the audit procedures, external auditors lament a delay in this regulatory intervention, due to the inability of the regulators to keep up with the pace of technological innovation:

> *The industry is running faster than the regulators: unless the rule setter updates the standards considering new technologies, audit procedures and evidence, the profession will continue to run behind.*
>
> (Survey – Auditor 81)

As a result, regulators' actions are a matter of concern for the future of the profession and subject to a trade-off between increasing the monitoring and scrutiny over the audit profession and sustaining the innovations and changes in the audit practice. Indeed, it seems that regulators are more preoccupied with controlling and reducing the risks of audit fraud by increasing controls and scrutiny, instead of supporting the implementation of new technologies in the audit practice, which in turn may naturally reduce the risks of fraud and errors. Further, regulators should probably encourage the implementation of new technologies and play a more active role, as the introduction and regulation of data analytics in audit may facilitate the continuous monitoring of the profession for regulators.

8.4 The future of small practitioners

The technological changes initiated in the audit profession, as well as the consequent regulatory interventions, may impact the future existence and strategies of small practitioners. Indeed, already in the aftermath of the 2014 EU audit reform, the interview participants indicated that the regulatory requirements have fostered an increase in the internal controls and risk management of auditors, which entails higher expenses for the audit firms. As a result, it is predicted that while the Big Four will be able to sustain such an increase in costs, smaller practitioners will be required to find alternative solutions or merge, thereby fostering further concentration in the industry. The larger structure of the Big Four auditors allows them to bear the additional costs. However, this will be a reason for strategic change for small auditors:

> *My expectation is that the single auditors (small) will progressively disappear, because it's clear that if they (even the smallest auditors) I must also have a quality control system, it becomes a little difficult for a small auditor to keep up. So, potentially, single auditors will need to merge. And I would also expect a certain specialisation, which is accountants who will decide to focus on a certain service but adopting a similar business model as medium or big auditors.*
>
> (Big Four auditor, Milan, 2018)

Both Big Four and non-Big Four auditors openly recognise that there are a few non-Big Four audit firms that are growing or specialising to overcome the limitations intrinsic to their small size, while other audit firms are simply too small to be in the position of providing auditing services adequate for the new EU requirements. These smaller firms may decide to focus on niches where they can become advisory experts.

Survey participants indicated a limitation in the technological development within audit, as the introduction of data analytics and digital tools will require costly initial investments that may be unsustainable for small auditors:

> *Not all auditors (especially the smaller ones) are capable of investing in the emerging technologies.*
>
> (Survey – Auditor 39)

However, some respondents working in smaller firms underline how via specialisation, smaller firms can be more effective in implementing new audit technologies than bigger firms because smaller firms are less subject to the imposition of certain corporate information systems from the top. As a result, there is also the opportunity for smaller firms to champion specific audit technologies or even construct more advanced software to sustain audit procedures. As a result, the ongoing regulatory and technological changes are opening different possible scenarios for smaller firms, if they are capable to navigate and be strategic in an increasingly competitive market setting.

8.5 The attractiveness of the audit profession

The decreasing attractiveness of the audit profession and its inability to retain the best and brightest young auditors have been a concern already raised by past auditing research (Houghton et al., 2010), especially if one cares to consider that the retention of competent auditors may ensure higher audit quality. Our more recent research has collected the perceptions of auditors with regard to the attractiveness of the profession, the skills lacking or present in the entry-level auditors, and the motivations for which young auditors are leaving or are staying in the audit profession.

The initial insights from the exploratory interviews seem to confirm the loss of attractiveness of the profession due to the lack of intellectual challenges needed to keep bright, high-achieving, young auditors. The tick-the-boxes compliance approach of audit does not empower auditors to use more judgement, and they tend to follow more routine, dull approaches to audit that do not resolve the concerns raised by past studies on this issue.

> *This big drive for greater quality is likely, to lead in the end to lower quality because it will drive out the brightest people from audit and the net result is you'll end up with audits which tick the boxes and applying no real intellectual challenge or limited intellectual challenge.*
>
> (Non-Big Four auditor, London, 2018)

However, this is not a general opinion, as European auditors appear to be divided about the attractiveness of the profession and the ability to retain the brightest young professionals. Indeed, half of the survey participants (49%) agree or strongly agree that the audit profession attracts the best and the brightest of young auditors, but another solid portion of respondents (38%) disagree or strongly disagree and point to the lack of intellectual challenge as the reason for this loss of attractiveness of the profession. Some of the open-ended comments also support this view:

> *In the first years of experience the work is not exciting, and the most interesting aspects and the remuneration are too distant in the view of the new generations.*
>
> (Survey – Auditor 27)

From the initial interviews, auditors also indicated the increasing relevance of data analysis skills as a fundamental requirement for new graduates willing to enter the profession. They also showed the expectation that universities start aligning their teaching contents to improve data analysis skills of graduates, which has been happening in the past few years (Kend and Nguyen, 2020). Such requirement has been largely confirmed by the surveyed European auditors, who agree (59%) and strongly agree (35%) that data analysis skills are becoming more and more relevant for the audit profession. In addition, the survey participants seem to appreciate the preparation of young auditors where data analysis and IT tools are concerned. Many agree (41%) and strongly agree (17%) that the background skills of young auditors are up to speed with the new technologies available in audit, thereby confirming the reliance of more senior auditors on young colleagues around emerging technologies:

> *[...] our younger colleagues are experts in the use of the technological tools through which we can carry out the new audit activities.*
>
> (Big Four auditor, Milan, 2018)

However, while the audit professionals in Europe seem to appreciate the contribution of the younger generation, there is still a good portion of young auditors leaving the profession. Our survey also investigated the motivations that can push young and bright auditors to leave and move to a different sector. Several comments indicate that the most frequent motivations are the heavy workload, the long hours, and the stressful environment that are not matched with an adequate remuneration and career prospects. Some participants also point to the lack of work-life balance because of the heavy workloads and poor pay. Further, when faced with stress, people tend to leave, thereby generating a vicious circle where those remaining need to deal with increased workloads because firms are understaffed.

> *The workload as staff capacities is not realistic resulting in understaffing and heavy workload for those that are at the firm.*
>
> (Survey – Auditor 1)

> *The audit profession is hard, the rhythms are frenetic, flexible hours, work life balance is not permitted, and the work is not well paid for the actual hours you work.*
>
> (Survey – Auditor 10)

> *There is a very high level of pressure in the work, and it is not easy to find a good work-life balance.*
>
> (Survey – Auditor 38)

> *The auditor's lifestyle does not allow much free time and the working hours are more than the ones established in the work contract and they are not paid.*
>
> (Survey – Auditor 39)

> *Lack of work life balance and salary not aligned with the increasing cost of living.*
>
> (Survey – Auditor 62)

However, survey participants also recognised that there are advantages and positive aspects to enter and stay in the audit profession. In particular, the learning experience that young auditors can make in the first years is perceived as highly relevant and attainable in a very short time, thereby benefitting their future career prospects within the finance sector. Several comments underline the wide range of professional skills that can be learnt in the audit profession:

> *It provides the most holistic view of the finance industry that makes them relevant to enter other job markets within finance.*
>
> (Survey – Auditor 1)

> *In the first years of experience, it is granted a quick understanding of different aspects of the auditing, accounting and finance context.*
>
> (Survey – Auditor 27)

> *Young auditors enter the profession for the young and dynamic environment, for the opportunities to learn quickly, for the variety of experiences offered by an audit career, for the value that work experience at a big 4 company still has on a young person's CV.*
>
> (Survey – Auditor 29)

> *They can improve their knowledge in a short time and open their professional mind.*
>
> (Survey – Auditor 73)

It is, however, concerning how some comments considering the positive aspects of staying in the audit profession also underline that the profession is starting to lose its appeal. In our view, this is not a problem limited to the audit profession and related to the specific characteristics of the profession. Rather, this is a larger problematic that interests several sectors and industries. Indeed, the recent COVID-19 pandemic has increased professionals' awareness about the importance of their work-life balance and has induced younger generations to leave their jobs if they were not considerate of their work-life balance. As a result, while the audit profession must make some changes to become more appealing for younger and brighter auditors and graduates, it is also important to factor in the increasing desire of professionals in every sector – especially the most stressful ones – to improve their work-life balance conditions.

8.6 Future of the audit profession: perceptions on the next five years

As part of the interview protocol, participants were typically asked a final question about the future of the audit profession. In the UK, most comments about the future centred around the implications of the UK leaving the EU due to Brexit. At the end, the UK officially left the EU bloc on 31 January 2020, and a 11-month transition phase begun, running to 31 December 2020. Thus, a 43-year-old relationship was ended when Britain left the EU. The impact of Brexit on the audit profession in the UK remains under investigation from the UK Parliament (since 2019). The notion of critical juncture is well established in institutional theory and refers to "situations of uncertainty in which decisions of important actors are causally decisive for the selection of one path of institutional development over other possible paths" (Capoccia, 2016). Brexit currently represents a critical juncture for the UK (*The Guardian*, 2021). There is little doubt that Brexit is a major disruption to the UK in recent history and that it is clearly a matter of much general interest, not just academic interest. The UK accountancy and auditing sector plays a vital role in the growth and success of all industries and economic activities in the UK and the EU. It is important to address the impact of Brexit on the UK professional market for audit and assurance services, as it could have implications for other jurisdictions, related to the supply of skilled labour and professional accounting services, and regulatory reform. At this point in time the longer-term effects of Brexit have not had time to come into effect at the local economy level. For instance, the soft border between Northern Ireland (in the UK) and the Republic of Ireland (in the EU) remains a major issue for the UK government (Basioudis and Kend, 2022).

The participants in this study indicated future concerns related to Brexit and how the UK and various corporates will handle the UK leaving the EU. The concerns relate to: (1) the UK's loss of influence in the EU related to accounting and auditing developments; and (2) the UK being given fair treatment after it leaves the EU. The following comments from participants highlight concerns raised in this study:

> *In the UK, at least currently, maybe post Brexit will change how businesses operate and where they operate, but at the moment so many of our businesses are integrally involved in the European market that*

> *there will be a natural – unless that fundamentally changes, there will be a natural desire to be on the same playing field, level playing field.*
>
> (Big Four auditor, London, 2018)

During the interviews conducted in 2018, the issue was raised that after the UK leaves the EU, citizens from other Member States will have to apply for immigration status in the UK because freedom of movement will end, and they will no longer be able to come and go in an unrestricted manner. This raises interesting future questions about the role of place and migration in the process, and whether UK auditors will be treated the same. There has been heightened fear that Euro non-membership could leave the UK audit profession at the mercy of rules set predominately by a group that does not consider the UK's best interests. The main worry for the UK is that the EU countries could use their numerical advantage to dominate:

> *So, I suppose within the European Union, I think the main issue will be the perception issue, will UK accountants be seen as less European, and so less in demand. Yeah, I think that's an issue.*
>
> (Non-Big Four auditor, London, 2018)

In relation to specific EU audit reforms such as the provision of non-audit services (NAS) by auditors to their audit clients, auditor firm rotation, and independence (EU Audit Reform, 2014a, 2014b), it appears that the UK will continue with these rules and codes for the time being. Calls for a full structural break-up of the audit firms is currently being considered by the UK government. There is a need for greater clarity on certain aspects of the EU audit reform agenda, and Brexit may potentially provide time for reflection as some areas can be revisited and clarified, which may eventually impact the material carriers of institutional practices like the ISAs or the relevant professional codes (Basioudis and Kend, 2022).

8.7 Summary

We know little about how changes in the COVID-19 environment affect audit tasks completed by external auditors (including judgements on what to include in external audit reports). Thus, even above and beyond the EU audit reforms, Brexit, and many of the other challenges mentioned in this chapter (such as staff retention), external auditors face new challenges brought on by factors well beyond the control of governments and financial market regulators more generally. The profession is becoming less attractive to young graduates, who are staying less and less in the profession. To change this trend audit firms will need to grant a better work-life balance and more rewarding remunerations, especially if they want to attract young talent with the necessary skills to navigate the digital revolution that is already impacting the profession. A decade ago, we had the GFC to contend with, and now the COVID-19 pandemic. External auditors will rise to the latest challenges as they have always tended to do so. For instance, external auditors responded appropriately to the GFC in the past, a view supported by several international studies (Xu et al., 2013; Geiger et al., 2014). Therefore, we have reason to believe that external auditors can meet new challenges in the future as they appear.

Note

1 The insights have been collected via the interviews and the survey that are described in Chapter 7. Please refer to the Section 7.3, Research methodology, of Chapter 7 for more details regarding how data have been collected and analysed. To summarise, during exploratory interviews in 2018 with auditors in Italy and the UK some insights about the future of the audit profession were gathered and further investigated with a survey in early 2022. The survey has asked more in-depth questions to enlarge the findings from the initial interviews. In this chapter we share the insights from the interviews and the survey where auditors shared their hopes and concerns for the future of the profession.

References

Albitar, K., Gerged, A., Kikhia, H., and Hussainey, K. (2021). Auditing in times of social distancing: The effect of COVID-19 on auditing quality. *International Journal of Accounting & Information Management,* 29(1): 169–178.

Basioudis, I., and Kend, M. (2022). *The impacts of Brexit on the audit and assurance services market in the U.K.: An exploratory study of stakeholder perceptions.* Working paper, RMIT University.

Brydon, D. (2019). *Assess, assure, and inform: Improving audit quality and effectiveness.* The UK Government.

Capoccia, G. (2016). Critical junctures. In Fioretos, O., Falleti, T., and Sheingate, A. (Eds.), *The Oxford handbook of historical institutionalism* (pp. 89–106). Oxford: Oxford University Press.

Competition & Market Authority—CMA (2018). *Statutory audit services market study.* London: National Archives.

De Martinis, M., and Burrowes, A.W. (1996). Materiality and risk judgements: A review of users' expectations. *Managerial Finance,* 22(9): 16–34.

Department for Business, Energy, and Industrial Strategy (2021). *Restoring trust in audit and corporate governance: Consultation on the government's proposals.* March, CP382.

European Union (EU) (2014a). Directive 2006/43/EC of the European Parliament and of the Council of 17 May 2006 on statutory audits of annual accounts and consolidated accounts. Available at: https://eur-lex.europa.eu/legal-content/EN/TXT/HTML/?uri=CELEX:32014L0056&from=EN. Accessed 15.03.19.

European Union (EU) (2014b). Regulation (EU) No 537/2014 of the European parliament and of the council of 16 April 2014 on specific requirements regarding statutory audit of public-interest entities and repealing Commission Decision 2005/909/EC. Available at: http://eur-lex.europa.eu/legal-content/EN/TXT/PDF/?uri=CELEX:32014R0537&from=EN. Accessed 15.03.19.

Geiger, M.A., Raghunandan, K., and Riccardi, W. (2014). The global financial crisis: US Bankruptcies and going-concern audit opinions. *Accounting Horizons,* 28(1): 59–75.

The Guardian (2021). UK-Germany trade slumps amid Brexit and COVID fallout. *The Guardian Online,* 10 March 2021. https://www.theguardian.com/uk-news/2021/mar/09/uk-germany-trade-slumps-brexit-covid. Accessed on 10.12.21.

Houghton, K.A., Jubb, C., Kend, M., and Ng, J. (2010). *The future of audit: Keeping capital markets efficient.* ANU E Press.

Humphrey, C., and Moizer, P. (1990). From techniques to ideologies: An alternative perspective on the audit function. *Critical Perspectives on Accounting,* 1(3): 217–238.

Humphreys, K., and Trotman, K.T. (2022). Judgment and decision-making research on CSR reporting in the COVID-19 pandemic environment. *Accounting and Finance,* 62(1), 739–765. https://doi.org/10.1111/acfi.12805

Kend, M., and Nguyen, L.A. (2020). Big data analytics and other emerging technologies: The impact on the Australian audit and assurance profession. *Australian Accounting Review,* 30: 269–282.

Kend, M., Leoni, G., Florio, C., and Gaia, S. (2021). *EU audit reforms: Analysing different impacts in the UK and Italy.* London: ICAEW.

Kingman, J. (2018, December). *Independent review of the Financial Reporting Council – Final Report.*

Koh, H.C., and Woo, E. (1998). The expectations gap in auditing. *Managerial Auditing Journal,* 13(3): 147–154.

Porter, B. (1993). An empirical study of the audit expectation-performance gap. *Accounting and Business Research,* 24: 49–68.

Samiolo, R. (2012). Commensuration and styles of reasoning: Venice, cost–benefit, and the defence of place. *Accounting Organisations and Society,* 37: 382–402.

Xu, Y., Carson, E., Fargher, N., and Jiang, L. (2013). Responses by Australian auditors to the global financial crisis. *Accounting and Finance,* 53(1): 303–338.

Index

Note: **Bold** page numbers refer to tables; *italic* page numbers refer to figures and page numbers followed by "n" denote endnotes.